I0510385

Financial Focus

FIVE COMMON MISTAKES RETIREES MAKE AND HOW TO PREVENT THEM

Robert D. Cooper

Robert Cooper & Associates
KERNERSVILLE, NORTH CAROLINA

Copyright © 2018 by Robert D. Cooper.

All rights reserved. No part of this publication may be reproduced, distributed or transmitted in any form or by any means, including photocopying, recording, or other electronic or mechanical methods, without the prior written permission of the publisher, except in the case of brief quotations embodied in critical reviews and certain other noncommercial uses permitted by copyright law. For permission requests, write to the publisher at the address below.

Robert D. Cooper/Robert Cooper & Associates
935 East Mountain St., Suite E
Kernersville, NC 27284
www.coopercares.com

Book layout ©2013 BookDesignTemplates.com

Financial Focus/ Robert D. Cooper. —1st ed.
ISBN 978-1717216304

Robert Cooper & Associates is an independent financial services firm that helps individuals create retirement strategies using a variety of investment and insurance products to custom suit their needs and objectives. Investment advisory services offered only by duly registered individuals through AE Wealth Management (AEWM). AEWM and Robert Cooper & Associates are not affiliated companies.

The contents of this book are provided for informational purposes only and are not intended to serve as the basis for any financial decisions. Any tax, legal or estate planning information is general in nature. It should not be construed as legal or tax advice. Always consult an attorney or tax professional regarding the applicability of this information to your unique situation.

Information presented is believed to be factual and up-to-date, but we do not guarantee its accuracy and it should not be regarded as a complete analysis of the subjects discussed. All expressions of opinion are those of the author as of the date of publication and are subject to change. Content should not be construed as personalized investment advice nor should it be interpreted as an offer to buy or sell any securities mentioned. A financial advisor should be consulted before implementing any of the strategies presented.

Investing involves risk, including the potential loss of principal. No investment strategy can guarantee a profit or protect against loss in periods of declining values. Any references to protection benefits or guaranteed/lifetime income streams generally refer to fixed insurance products, never securities or investment products. Insurance and annuity product guarantees are backed by the financial strength and claims-paying ability of the issuing insurance company.

Contents

Preface v

Where Are You on the Tape Measure of Life? 1

The Three Phases of Your Financial Life...................... 13

The Times, They Are A-Changin' 25

FIVE COMMON RETIREMENT MISTAKES 35

    Mistake No. 1: Investing As Though You're Still Working
.... 37

    Mistake No. 2: Not Protecting Yourself From a Significant
Financial Loss 41

    Mistake No. 3: Not Guaranteeing Your Basic Income
Needs 51

    Mistake No. 4: Not Paying Attention to Your Portfolio
Costs 63

    Mistake No. 5: Not Knowing How Much Money You
Need in Retirement... 75

Life Insurance as a Retirement Income Tool................ 81

In-Service Rollovers: The 401(k) "Escape Hatch"......... 91

Money Zones: Red Money, Green Money and Hybrid Zone....... 99

Choosing the Right Financial Advisor for You 109

About the Author 115

Acknowledgments 119

Contact..121

To my brother, Clarence Bennett Cooper, Jr. (a.k.a. "Buck"). Buck passed away May 31, 2017. During his life, he had many struggles. Buck served our country by doing two tours of duty in the Vietnam War, where he served as a medic. He was a quiet and humble man who, in his later years, learned to trust Christ and found pleasure in helping others.

Preface

I was a student at Catawba College in Salisbury, North Carolina, when I came home one day to pay my parents a surprise visit. As I opened the front door and stepped inside, I heard raised voices. I couldn't help but overhear them. They were arguing over money. What I heard would change my life forever.

"Eight thousand dollars down the tubes! How could you have done that?" my mother, Jenelle Cooper was saying to Clarence Cooper, my father.

The year was 1981. My father was a construction worker and my mother worked at a local textile mill. They weren't rich, but they were hard workers and diligent savers. By pinching pennies for 30 years, they had managed to save a little over $200,000 for their retirement, which was, at that time, about 10 years away.

When Dad decided to seek investment advice, the first place he thought of was his local bank. Clarence Cooper was a pretty smart man. He could build a house almost single-handedly. He could read a blueprint and understand what all the lines and squiggles meant. He was thoroughly familiar with the plumbing and electrical systems that went into a building. But he knew little about investing money. The financial advisor at the bank had told my father that he should invest in a mutual fund. And so, he did.

Maybe the bank's advisor did point out that the mutual fund had a 5 percent front-end load, and maybe he didn't. Either way, it probably went over Dad's head. Dad knew about front loaders, but I doubt he would have understood what "front-end load" meant. It meant when he sank $160,000 of his and my mother's hard-earned money into the fund, $8,000 came right off the top for commissions, fees and expenses before the investment would earn a penny. I'm sure he didn't understand that; hence, the argument.

My mother discovered this shocking fact when she opened the first statement and was alarmed to see the balance was $8,000 less than the original amount invested. My father agreed to go down to the bank the next morning to find out why the money had vanished. That's when he was shown the fine print that explained about the front-end load.

"That's the way these things work," the advisor said, trying to reassure him. "Just hang in there! You will make that back in no time."

So, Clarence Cooper hung in there, figuring he had no choice. He had already signed the papers, hadn't he? Still, he felt taken advantage of. My mother, although disappointed, worried and skeptical, also let it go, chalking it up to experience. My father passed away a few years later without ever having recouped the loss.

Keep in mind, this was 1981. If you remember those days, interest rates on certificates of deposit (CDs) were running in the double digits then. The advisor could have directed my parents toward a CD in which the principal would be guaranteed, and they would have earned between 10–12 percent in the first year. Plus, the bank might have even given him a free toaster as a premium!

An Eye-Opener

After hearing their fearful struggle over the mutual fund incident, I returned to college to complete my degree in business and economics. I was determined to get to the bottom of what had happened to my parents. What an epiphany it was when I learned financial advisors worked under two standards — **suitability** and **fiduciary.** I discovered many banks, insurance companies and investment companies are subject to only a "suitability" standard when dispensing financial advice.

To explain the difference, imagine you are shopping for a new automobile. The first place you stop is a Chevrolet dealership. You describe what you are looking for in a new car: excellent gas mileage, leather seats, hatchback, anti-lock brakes, four-wheel-drive, rear-view camera, video player, heated seats, etc. And the price needs to be under $29,000.

It could be the car you described is sitting not at the Chevrolet dealership, but three blocks away at the Ford store. But the salesperson leads you over to a car on the Chevrolet showroom floor that has *most* of the attributes you are looking for, and explains to you the price is *almost* within your budget. The salesperson makes the sale and gets the commission. You didn't get exactly what you wanted, but you have a car that will get you from point A to point B and is therefore **suitable** for your needs.

The **fiduciary** standard legally obligates the financial advisor to work in the **best interests** of the **client** — without regard to commission or personal remuneration. Using the automobile dealership analogy, under the fiduciary standard, the salesperson would listen carefully to take note of each detail on your wish list, thoroughly research the matter, and then tell you that the car you need is three blocks away down at the Ford dealership. (Disclaimer: I am neither a Ford nor a Chevy fan. Just using the names to make a point.)

In the case of my father, investing in a stock mutual fund when he was 10 years away from retirement, while not necessarily "unsuitable," was not in his best interests, especially with CDs paying double-digit interest rates. That $8,000 off-the-top charge was certainly unwarranted. Other mutual funds were available at the time with little or no upfront charges. Also, his and my mother's life's savings were at risk in the stock market at a time when they were fast approaching retirement. Their money had not been easy to come by. Losing $8,000 represented a year's worth of scrimping and saving.

I would learn, had the bank been operating under the higher "fiduciary" standard, it would have been legally bound to disclose and discuss all fees, and recommend only what was in the best interests of my father.

On April 6, 2016, the United States Department of Labor released new regulations to force all financial advisors to work in the best interests of their clients. *Thanks*, Uncle Sam! Long overdue!

Under the new ruling, if an advisor steered a person seeking advice on a qualified retirement account in a direction clearly not in his or her best interests, that advisor would be breaking the law. This would stop some, but probably not all, financial salespeople from "hawking their wares" strictly to line their own pockets. If the new rules reach implementation, anyone who hangs out a "financial advisor" shingle will be required to listen carefully to clients, discerning each one's unique financial situation, and making recommendations that match — something they should have been doing all along. Unfortunately, some financial lobbyists have been successful in having the DOL rule delayed, so we have yet to see if it will ever be fully implemented.

The bottom line: It is imperative financial advice fit the person receiving it.

Can you imagine walking into a shoe store, asking to try on a pair of shoes, and having the following conversation with the salesperson?

"I would like to try these on in size 10."

"We have those shoes, but only in size 8."

"But I wear size 10!"

"Size 8 will be OK. You see, they will stretch the more you wear them. That will be $100, please."

Insane, right? Yet millions of Americans settle for financial planning that fits them as poorly as improperly sized shoes.

As I write this book, I have almost three decades' experience in helping people find their way through the maze of financial decisions they must make when they approach retirement. I could tell you horror stories, most of which are the result of unsuspecting, naïve, trusting folks following errant advice, some of which was the result of uneducated advisors who unwittingly led them astray. In other cases, however, I can draw no other conclusion than that it was purposeful and done with a profit motive.

One reason I decided to write this book is to focus the bright spotlight of truth and full disclosure on the latter. My aim is to expose some of the more blatant efforts to circumvent the fiduciary mandate.

I also happen to believe an educated investor is a more successful investor. I want to provide baby boomers who are approaching retirement with alternative investment strategies that can spare them the kind of heartache my parents experienced and show them practical ways of not outliving their resources in retirement.

If you bought this book anticipating a get-rich-quick scheme, or "10 hot stock tips that can't lose," I apologize for the disappointment. That's not what you will find here, and if you see me personally, I will refund the purchase price of your book. What you *will* find in this book are practical solutions to real-life problems facing retirees. Some of these solutions might be unfamiliar to you. Please don't let that derail you. Read on. Or, as they say in the new computer age, "scroll down to the bottom of the page" before automatically kicking a nontraditional idea to the curb. Just as some of the best scenery on any road trip lies off the beaten path, some of the most effective ways to build and protect wealth in today's fast-changing economic climate are outside established paradigms. I have heard it called, "thinking outside the box." I think you will see what I mean as we move forward. Thank you, dear reader, for joining me on this journey.

CHAPTER ONE

Where Are You on the Tape Measure of Life?

"The good life is one inspired by love and guided by knowledge."
~ Bertrand Russell

Nearly every household has a retractable tape measure. It features a yellow concave blade with inches clearly marked. The curve in the blade allows you to extend the tape quite a distance away from yourself before it collapses. That's good for measuring in open space. It's also good for illustrating a point I like to make in the financial seminars I conduct from time to time.

As I extend the steel tape from the cassette, I explain to the audience that each inch represents a year of our lives. It is easy to visualize life this way — how long you have lived, how much longer you will live.

As hard as I try, and as steadily as I hold the tape while extending it, I can never get it to go past the 100-inch mark before the curved metal blade buckles and collapses to the floor. Try it yourself; you'll see what I mean. Of course, none of us needs reminding we are mere mortals with an expiration date. But, unless you have just returned from a doctor's office with some bad news, you don't know exactly what that expiration date is. All you can do is guess.

The Bible puts the average human lifespan at between 70 and 80. "The span of our life is 70 years, or 80 if one is especially strong." (Psalms 90:10, New World Translation). By the way, that verse is an excerpt from a prayer of Moses — famous for receiving the 10 Commandments and parting the Red Sea. The Good Book says he lived to be 120, so he must have been especially strong.

The plain fact is, people are living longer these days. Life expectancy in the 21st century has increased dramatically over previous centuries. Most babies born in 1900, for example, didn't live beyond 50 years of age. In the 18th century, few people reached what we would call "old age" today. Parasitic disease and illness from infections were common. In the 20th century, medical science took a giant leap forward. Vaccines became available, giving millions immunity from such childhood diseases as polio, measles and smallpox. Couple that with cleaner drinking water, more sanitary living standards and better nutrition, and you have the formula for the longer lifespans we are enjoying today.

Elderly Living Longer

According to the U.S. Census Bureau, one thing demographers did not anticipate was an increase in survival in the older age groups. A report published March 28, 2016, says, "Population aging ... reflects a human success story of increased longevity. Today, living to age 70 or age 80 is no longer a rarity in many parts of the world." The way longevity statistics work, the longer you live, the longer you will live. In other words, if you make it to age

70, your chances of reaching age 90 are better. There are several studies on this with lots of facts and figures. But most of them give a 60-year-old an average of 22 to 23 more years of life. Keep in mind, that's *average*. And you know what they say about averages — put one foot in ice water and the other foot in boiling water, and *on average* you are comfortable. Averages take into consideration those who live to be 100, as well as those who die early in accidents.

The NIA says the elderly population is the fastest-growing segment of the world's population, "from 2025 to 2050, the older population is projected to almost double to 1.6 billion globally, whereas the total population will grow by just 34 percent over the same period."[1]

OK, Robert. So, what's all that got to do with the price of tea in China? Well it speaks to a very real concern that most people have — *outliving their resources*. On the one hand, living a long, fruitful and rewarding life is a great thing. On the other, if you aren't financially prepared, it could mean your money won't last as long as you do. That means you could end up becoming a burden on your loved ones or a ward of the state in your old age. That is something no one wants. Some surveys say that is what people fear most as they age. More than snakes, spiders or even dying.

The financial information website, MarketWatch, ran a piece July 21, 2016 entitled "Older People Fear This More than Death," pointing out what scares people most about retirement. Author Catey Hill writes: "It's not being bored, unable to travel or even death itself that scares older Americans most about retirement —

---

[1] Wan He, Daniel Goodkind and Paul Kowal. United States Census Bureau. March 28, 2016. "An Aging World: 2015."
https://www.census.gov/library/publications/2016/demo/P95-16-1.html.

it's running out of money." Some excerpts from her article are as follows:[2]

- "More than 6 out of 10 feared running out of money before they died more than death itself."
- "A poll of 2,000 workers over the age of 50 said their greatest fear about retirement was outliving their savings and investments."
- "57% of financial planners surveyed reported that the top concern for their clients was running out of money."

When baby boomers read articles telling them they will likely outlive their parents' generation, their first reaction might be a "Yes!" and a fist pump. Then they do a little math and calculate how much is in their 401(k) or savings accounts, and then the anxiety sets in.

Hill writes, "This is exacerbated by the fact that "during their careers, boomers saw the significant decline and, in many cases elimination of traditional pension plans, removing a significant source of guaranteed and ongoing income that their parents enjoyed in retirement."

She also points out baby boomers, because they expect to have a more active retirement than their parents, will simply need more money to do what they want to do in retirement. More and more, the mental picture boomers have of retirement is different from that of their parents. Most of them do not see themselves in rocking chairs on the front porch like Ma and Pa Kettle. Instead of sedentary lifestyles in retirement, most 60-somethings see themselves playing golf or tennis, or boarding planes to visit faraway places.

---

[2] Catey Hill. MarketWatch. July 21, 2016. "Older People Fear This More than Death." https://www.marketwatch.com/story/older-people-fear-this-more-than-death-2016-07-18.

In the MarketWatch article, Hill says people in their 50s have only saved an average of $117,000 for retirement. Most experts say that's not nearly enough. A Fidelity Viewpoints piece published March 16, 2016, says we should try to have at least one times our income at age 30, three times our income at age 40, seven times our income at age 55 and 10 times our income at age 67. That means that if, by age 55, you are earning $70,000 per year, you should have around $490,000 saved up. When you are 67, you should have $700,000 in savings. Other experts say those numbers are a little low.[3]

Human nature being what it is, most people don't start thinking seriously about retirement until they hit the half-century mark.

"A TransAmerica survey showed that only about one in three people in their 50s say that saving for retirement is their greatest financial priority," writes Hill, adding that for the majority, their priority is covering basic living expenses and trying to pay down debt.

Here's another statistic I found troubling: Of those employees offered a 401(k) or similar retirement program, only one in three are contributing more than 10 percent of their income to it.

Whenever I talk to young people about their financial futures, I implore them to save as much as possible in their younger years. I encourage them to contribute the maximum to retirement programs offered by their employers, *especially if matching funds are available.*[4]

---

[3] Fidelity. June 5, 2017. "How Much Do I Need to Save for Retirement?" https://www.fidelity.com/viewpoints/retirement/how-much-money-do-i-need-to-retire.

[4] Catey Hill. MarketWatch. July 21, 2016. "Older People Fear This More than Death." https://www.marketwatch.com/story/older-people-fear-this-more-than-death-2016-07-18.

Avocado Toast

Multi-millionaire Australian real estate magnate Tim Gurner made news in May 2017 when he advised millennials (those born between 1982 and 2004) to stop spending foolishly and save more. He said indulging in extravagance is the main reasons why young people can't afford to own a home.

Gurner told the Australian news show "60 Minutes," "When I was trying to buy my first home, I wasn't buying smashed avocado for $19 and four coffees at $4 each."

At the time of Gurner's remarks, the price of avocados had doubled because of high demand and slack production. But he witnessed many young people splurging on the expensive treat at restaurants like Starbucks and Chipotle.

"Money Magazine" amplified the comments in an article entitled, "Millionaire to Millennials: Stop Buying Avocado Toast If You Want to Buy a Home," in which Australian columnist Bernard Salt noted that the cost of the avocado-and-coffee treats multiplied several times a week could make a nice down payment on a house.[5]

Personally, I'm not a big fan of avocados. Perhaps it is an acquired taste. But I must agree with Gurner and Salt in the saving versus spending debate. You can either have the immediate satisfaction of what money can buy, or you can have the money. But you can't have both. Saving money is good. Saving money and investing it is better. Investing with compound interest is better still.

---

[5] Jennifer Calfas. Time. May 15, 2017. "Millionaire to Millennials: Stop Buying Avocado Toast If You Want to Buy a Home." http://time.com/money/4778942/avocados-millennials-home-buying/.

The Eighth Wonder of the World

Albert Einstein reportedly said, "Compound interest is the eighth wonder of the world. He who understands it, earns it. He who doesn't, pays it."

As a kid growing up in central North Carolina, we didn't get much snow — maybe once or twice a year. When we did, it was a grand holiday. Schools would close at the virtual mention of the white stuff, and as soon as the flakes began to fall, grocery store shelves would be denuded of staples like milk, bread and eggs. Most of the time, it was only an inch or two. But for us kids, it was time to make snowmen, and have snowball fights.

Compound interest reminds me of those snowballs we would roll across the lawn to make snowmen. They started small but, in the wet snow, the more we rolled them, the fatter they grew. Compound interest is that way. The interest begets interest, and then that interest begets even more interest, and before long, your original amount is overshadowed by the interest it has produced. You can imagine the effect created by regularly contributing to the account.

An avalanche starts small, but eventually develops unstoppable momentum.

Andrew Sather offers an excellent explanation of this phenomenon in his essay, "10 Reasons Why Compounding Interest Is the 8th Wonder of the World."

"Compounding interest can make you a millionaire, especially if you are young!" writes Sather. "Take the median income in the United States today: $50,000 a year. Now the average 25-year-old making $50,000 a year would only need to save and invest 10 percent and would have a staggering **$2,434,221** at 65!" This assumes a very optimistic 10 percent annual return in the stock market, which is certainly not guaranteed.[6]

Dollar-Cost Averaging

Young investors who are investing for the long-term can take advantage of a concept called dollar-cost averaging. If you invest the same small amount every pay period, you probably won't miss the money. And if you get into the habit of doing so, the rewards at the end of the trail (retirement day) can be phenomenal.

Since the secret of investing in the stock market is to buy low and sell high, it would be nice if you could time the market. Unfortunately, that is impossible. And if anyone tells you they can do so, they are either lying or delusional. But dollar-cost averaging allows you to purchase stocks at an "average" price when buying them on a regular schedule, both when the market is up and when it is down.

Let's say you send $50 every pay period to an investment account that automatically buys whatever number of shares in a mutual fund that $50 will buy. When the market is down, you buy more shares. That's a good thing. Those skinny shares will fatten up when the market rises. When the market is up, you buy fewer

---

[6] Andrew Sather. E Investing for Beginners. April 23, 2014. "10 Reasons Why Compounding Interest is the 8th Wonder of the World." http://einvestingforbeginners.com/compounding-interest.

shares, but that's OK, too. You are getting your money's worth. Dollar-cost averaging is generally most beneficial for younger investors who have plenty of time to ride the undulations of a volatile market.

Reverse Dollar-Cost Averaging

I guess this is as good a time as any to address another phenomenon called *reverse* dollar-cost averaging. As good as dollar-cost averaging can be for you while you are accumulating, *reverse* dollar-cost averaging can be a problem in your later years. When you retire, instead of making systematic deposits, you are likely making systematic *withdrawals*. Every time you make a withdrawal, you are selling shares in that mutual fund. Your expenses are likely constant, so you must sell as many shares as are necessary to come up with the same amount of cash each week. Since you need the same amount each week (or each month) to meet expenses, you can't wait until the market is on a roll to make your withdrawals. That way, higher share prices would mean more cash for fewer shares sold, and the rest of the account could continue growing. But, because you are now on a fixed income that must be produced by withdrawals from a market-based account, you have no choice but to sell the shares you must, *even if the market is tanking*. If you are in that situation, you are in the crosshairs of reverse dollar-cost averaging. Many folks who are in that area between a rock and a hard place are there because they did not take actions to ensure they had a steady and reliable source of income from financial vehicles that are protected from downside market risk.

Growing on Trees

One of the earliest financial maxims I can remember my father uttering was, "Money doesn't grow on trees, you know." I usually heard it after I asked him for some.

Maybe you remember the story of two brothers who lived during the Great Depression of the 1930s. The older brother, having heard there were jobs to be had in Chicago, hopped a train and proceeded there. In a letter to his younger brother, he advised him to drop everything and come to the Windy City to join him. "Money is growing on trees up here," he told him.

When the younger brother got to the big city, he sat on a park bench to take in the strange and wonderful sights of the place. Just then, a serendipitous gust of wind blew a dollar bill across his shoe tops. He started to bend over and pick it up, but then checked himself.

"Shucks," he said in an undertone. "I ain't gonna work on my first day in Chicago."

I found out very early in life that money indeed does not grow on trees. It must be earned by hard work. Perhaps that is why I have always been careful with it. By the age of 10, I was mowing our family's yard for $2 per week. I soon expanded to other neighborhood lawns. My little grass-cutting business soon grew to 20 customers and I kept it going all through college.

I can still remember the feeling I had when I walked into the local bank in Salisbury, North Carolina, to open a savings account. There were plenty of things I wanted to buy with the money I had in my wallet. But, because I had worked so hard for it, the inclination to save it was stronger than my urge to spend it. The good feeling I had from knowing I would have money in reserve was more valuable to me than the feeling of instant gratification I could have had by spending it.

Like most teenagers, when I turned 16, I wanted to own my own car. By then, I had accumulated enough money to make a down payment on a flashy new sports car. I would also have gone into years of debt, which I felt was even worse than spending hard-earned money! Instead, I bought a 13-year-old Chevy Impala for $200. It was a homely car that required a little work get into running condition. But I kept silently repeating the mantra to my-self: "OK, Robert. You can have what your money can buy, or you can have your money. But you can't have both."

Financial Decisions

Each purchase in life is a financial decision. My first real job af-ter graduating from college was with Food Lion, a large super-market chain headquartered in my hometown. Even though I was a store manager and in my 20s, I was still watching my pennies. I have a clear memory of working up a thirst on long, hard days. On the way out of the store, I had to walk past a Coke machine on the front of which was a larger-than-life picture of a bottle of Coca-Cola, glistening seductively, with droplets of water and small shards of ice clinging to it, looking as if it had that just that very moment been pulled from a cooler and offered to me. I remember dwelling momentarily on the image, considering the taste of the cool, refreshing liquid trickling down my parched throat. But each time, I would weigh whether I wanted to spend the 35 cents and treat myself, or keep the coins in my pocket and pass the machine by. Occasionally, I did buy a Coke. But usually I passed the ma-chine by, opting to keep the money.

I sometimes tell that story to audiences who attend my semi-nars to make the point that even small financial decisions are im-portant, not necessarily because of the amount of money involved, but because of the pattern they set. I also like to ask those in the audience for their opinion. Was I being a little too conservative? Maybe just a bit too frugal? I mean, after all, what impact on my financial goals could dropping a few coins into the Coke machine have made? Was I pushing parsimony a little too far? Well, per-haps I was. But when I tell them that, at age 22, I was able buy my own home, I hear low whistles and get a few looks of astonish-ment. I mention this, not to amaze or impress, but to make the point: Small things add up to big things in the end. Inches on a tape measure are composed of those tiny little marks representing eighths, 16ths and 32nds. Inches make feet and feet make yards. Similarly, dollars are made up of quarters, dimes, nickels and pennies. How you treat the lesser amounts reflects how you view larger amounts.

My conservative bent has served me well, both personally and professionally. In the decades I have spent helping other people with their money decisions, I have found clients are much more comfortable if their financial advisor has a conservative attitude. The reason is simple. It's *their* money!

Know Where You Are and Act Accordingly

Age wise, if you are on the 20-to-30-inch line of that measuring tape mentioned at the beginning of this chapter, develop the mindset of an aggressive saver and a wise investor. Make financial goals early and discipline yourself with steely-eyed focus to achieve them. Ignore the buy-now-pay-later beckoning of the Madison Avenue ad agencies, and buy only what you can afford here and now. Even then, give serious thought to whether it is a need or a want.

For those of us on the other end of the measuring tape — the ones they call baby boomers, born between 1946 and 1964 —we must know where we are in the financial stream of time. That means how we treat our wealth must match where we are on the timeline. That may mean making some dramatic changes, both in our spending behavior and our saving and investing behavior. To use a football analogy, when you are between the 20-yard line and the goal line, you play conservatively. Hug the ball tighter. Now, with retirement just a few years away, is no time to fumble. The road to a confident retirement is paved with prudent decisions that can be made only if we know where we are and where we are going.

CHAPTER TWO

The Three Phases of Your Financial Life

"A big part of financial freedom is having your heart and mind free from worry about the what-ifs of life."
~ Suze Orman

As a financial advisor, most of my time is focused on retirement income planning. Most of my clients are between the ages of 50 and 75. Most of these folks have gray hair and those little lines around the eyes we call "crow's feet," and other badges of wisdom they have earned throughout the years. Quite often, after working with them to develop a strategy for retirement, they ask me to talk to their adult children. The conversations I have with these younger adults are much different from the ones I have with their parents. They see the world differently. They aren't planning for retirement. Most of them are busy raising families, establishing careers, buying homes and filling them with furniture, thinking about the here and now. Their hourglass is top-heavy with sand and tomorrow seems a long way away.

A young couple sat in my office and, as is my custom, especially on first interviews, I let them do most of the talking. I learned about his work at a local equipment manufacturing firm. She was a stay-at-home mom, looking after their two small children. They had a medium-sized home in a nice neighborhood, two cars, three televisions and four credit cards, all of them with balances they intended to pay off within a year.

"How about savings?" I asked.

"Well," the wife said, "We are saving up for a trip to Disney World with the kids next summer."

"No, I mean savings for when the children are grown and gone, and you two are ready to retire," I said.

"Oh, I guess that's all taken care of," she said. "He has a 401(k) at work. And doesn't the government, like, take care of some of that?"

She turned to him, hoping he would elaborate. The husband just shrugged and said, "I guess they do, Honey." And then she turned to me and asked, "Don't they?"

I could see they had a lot to learn.

As we talked, I learned that his 401(k) plan at work was a "matching" plan, which meant the company offered to match a portion of what he contributed. But neither of them could tell me how much of his paycheck went into the plan, or, for that matter, what percentage the company matched. I suggested they bring a copy of his most recent 401(k) statement to our next meeting, and any paperwork that explained how his retirement plan was structured. That way, we could look at it together and figure it out.

This couple is somewhat typical of young families that are so busy with the day-to-day activities of their lives — PTA meetings, soccer practice, trips to the mall, etc. — they don't often focus past what's on their immediate horizon. To them, "retirement" is a word belonging to a place far removed from them in time. It's not yet real to them. But they do have one thing on their side — time. And it is perhaps the greatest of all their financial advantages.

At our next meeting, I learned his 401(k) had a very generous matching program. This couple is fortunate. Some companies offer no retirement savings plans whatsoever. Some offer 401(k)-type retirement plans, but don't match funds. There are all kinds of matching funds. In this case, for every dollar he put into the plan, his company was willing to put in a dollar, up to 5 percent of his gross pay for the year. I explained to them that if they did not contribute the maximum possible to his 401(k) plan, at least up to the amount his employer matches, they would be turning down "free money."

I also explained how dollar-cost averaging and compound interest could work for them. As is often the case, once they saw the light, they wanted to jump in with both feet.

"What if we want to save more money than the plan at work allows?" they asked. (For 2018, the annual maximum 401(k) contribution amount is $18,500.)

"Then you may want to open your own individual IRA," I said. "There will be no matching funds for such accounts, so make sure you maximize your contributions to the one at work first."

401(k)-type retirement plans are tax deferred. You are not taxed on money you contribute to the plan. Those taxes are deferred until you withdraw the money. Then you are taxed not only on the principal, but also on any gains.

I went on to explain the tax benefits of Roth IRAs.

"With the Roth plans, you contribute with taxed money, but after that, neither the gains nor the principal are ever taxed again." I suggested he make an appointment with the personnel department at his company to see if they offered a Roth 401(k). They are becoming more popular these days, and can be especially good for young people.

Finally, I encouraged them to get rid of their debt as soon as possible.

"Every dollar you owe is eroding your wealth," I told them. "While some debt may be unavoidable when you are building your lives, interest on debt erodes anything you build."

By the time the young couple left my office, I felt good about our discussions. Their awareness had been heightened about their future, and they had a better idea of what lay ahead of them, financially. From the window where I watch the world, most young families spend more time planning the details of a two-week vacation to the beach than they do planning the rest of their lives.

That this young couple is typical is borne out by statistics from the U.S. Census Bureau, which says two-thirds of all Americans don't contribute anything to a 401(k) or other retirement account available through their employer.

If you peel back the onion to find out why, most will say they just can't spare the cash it would take out of their paychecks. But according to an article published by Bloomberg, a New York financial media company, another reason is surfacing. Like the young couple in my office, many employees just don't understand their options. Often, they are given a folder with a pack of papers when they join a company, and they don't understand them. So, they may set them aside and forget them. Even large companies, which Bloomberg says are more apt to offer retirement plans, sometimes don't do a good enough job on educating their workers about the benefits of the plans and how they work.[7]

---

[7] Ben Steverman. Bloomberg. Feb. 21, 2017. "Two-Thirds of Americans Aren't Putting Money in Their 401(k)." https://www.bloomberg.com/news/articles/2017-02-21/two-thirds-of-americans-aren-t-putting-money-in-their-401-k.

FINANCIAL FOCUS | 17

Three Phases of Money

Just as our lives comprise phases—youth, adolescence, adulthood, etc.—our financial lives are composed of three distinct phases:

- **Accumulation**
- **Preservation**
- **Distribution**

The young couple I mentioned earlier were obviously in the accumulation phase. These are our younger years when we are working hard to earn, save and invest. We may take greater investment risks because we have time on our side. If our money is in a 401(k) or 403(b), it is most likely invested in mutual funds. Since mutual funds are based in the stock market, their shares will ebb and flow in value. If we are in the accumulation phase of our lives and we zip open the envelope containing our statement of these accounts and see a parenthesis indicating a loss of a few dollars during market downturns, there is no need to panic. Remember, dollar-cost averaging is working for you. Historically, it is usually two steps forward and one step back, then two more steps forward. The average annual return for the S&P 500 since its inception in 1928 is 9.8 percent, however, according to a CBNC article, "in the 89 years from 1928 to 2016, only six finished with a gain in [the 5 to 10 percent] range." This comes back to the idea of averages — some years, the index was quite high, with better than 20 percent in returns. Other years, bear markets prevailed.[8]

Losses Can Be Deceiving

Author Paul A. Merriman wrote the following in a Feb. 8, 2015, issue of the online magazine, MarketWatch:

---

[8] Michael Santoli. June 18, 2017. "The S&P 500 has already met its average return for a full year, but don't expect it to stay here." https://www.cnbc.com/2017/06/18/the-sp-500-has-already-met-its-average-return-for-a-full-year.html.

"Average returns, often a popular selling tool used by brokers and commission-based investment advisers, may sound good. But investors don't actually get average returns; they get compound returns. For example, if you invest $1,000 and it goes up 50 percent in the first year and then drops by 50 percent the second year, the average return was zero — leading some people to think you broke even. But you didn't. At the end of the first year you had $1,500; at the end of the second year you had only $750. That's a cumulative loss of 25 percent, or a compound loss of 13.4 percent a year."[9]

I sometimes ask audiences, "If I have $100,000 in the stock market and the market goes down 50 percent, what does the market have to go up for me to break even?" Most will answer 50 percent. On the surface, that math does sound right. You lost 50 percent, you got back 50 percent. Sounds like you should be back where you started, right? But when you think about it, when the market goes down 50 percent, you get a new starting point for the climb back up. You no longer have $100,000 in your account. When the market finally bottoms, you start the ride back up with $50,000, not $100,000.

So, how much would the market have to go up for you to get back to the $100,000 you started with? If it only went up 50 percent and stopped, you would be credited with only half of $50,000, or $25,000. That means you would have $75,000. To get back to even, you would need the market to go up another 25 percent. So, the answer to the original question, "How much must the market go back up again for me to break even?" is 100 percent, not 50 percent.

That is why it is so critical to avoid large investment losses. When you experience large losses, you have less to invest. It may

[9] Paul A. Merriman. Feb. 18, 2015. "Understanding Performance: The S&P 500 Index." https://www.marketwatch.com/story/understanding-performance-the-sp-500-in-2015-02-18.

take many years to get back to breakeven. In our examples here, we used 50 percent for easy math. But the truth is, losing 50 percent of your money in the market is an intolerable loss. Even *if* the market gained 10 percent per year, and you were 100 percent invested, it would take seven years (seven instead of 10 because of compounding) to get back to square one.

The accompanying chart shows how much you lost in a market slide on the left, and how much the market would have to rebound for you to break even. Why do we stop at 90 percent? Because, if you were to lose 100 percent, it's game over, isn't it folks?

Math of Gains and Losses	
If you lose…	You must make___ to get back to even.
5%	5%
10%	11%
15%	18%
20%	25%
25%	33%
30%	43%
35%	54%
40%	67%
45%	82%
50%	100%
75%	300%
90%	900%

To make the point even easier to grasp, I will sometimes take four quarters and place them on the table. This is you in the market just before a crash. The market loses 50 percent, you take two quarters away. The market rebounds 50 percent, you put one quarter back.

"Hey, where's the other quarter?" You will sometimes hear. But, if a moment of silence ensues, the light bulb clicks on. The market started its rebound when there were two quarters on deck. If it comes back 50 percent, I got half of those two quarters back, or 25 cents. That's the funny thing about math. It is always right. You can't argue with it.

Preservation Phase

Once the accumulation phase ends, the preservation phase begins. This is when you start thinking about retirement. It is no longer that faraway horizon. It is looming.

Here where we work and live in central North Carolina, what you see through the windshield of your car on a road trip is never more than 15 minutes away. It's not that way when you drive out west, where you catch sight of purple mountain ranges that are hundreds of miles and hours away. It seems to take forever for these vistas to finally emerge as real landscapes and for you to reach them. When you finally reach the foothills of these mountains and start to see just how massive they are, details start to appear, letting you know you have definitely left the plains and have quite a climb ahead of you.

In the accumulation phase of your financial life, it's only natural that you stay in the gear you're in, and don't alter your spending, saving and investing habits. But when you begin to enter the preservation zone, the changes you need to make become more apparent. Now you begin to think about retirement in earnest. You begin to develop mental pictures of what you will do once you leave the workforce.

Let's say you have been a good saver and a careful investor. What you *don't* want to do now is gamble with what you have accumulated. To use a Las Vegas term, you won't want to "double down" trying to make a big killing in the stock market. The odds are not in your favor.

Your goal now should be to hold on to what you have accumulated and be satisfied with reasonable growth. Remember those ebbs and flows that were no problem back when time was on your side? You don't want to get caught in one of those ebbs now. You may not have enough time to wait for the recovery. Your risk tolerance should be lower. And with good reason!

Distribution Phase

This is the financial phase of life when it is time to enjoy the fruits of your labor. It is a time when people spend their money the most judiciously because it is a finite resource. They are no longer receiving a paycheck, for one thing. Also, they realize that the less they spend, the more they will have working for them. It is the time when you begin collecting from your investments, not contributing to them. You start collecting using your investing and savings accounts to supplant the paycheck you used to receive every week. This is a big change, and it will continue the rest of your life. You are not building your wealth, but using it to fund your retirement.

If you have done it right, you will have paychecks and play checks. The paychecks cover your expenses and essentials, and play checks fund what you really want to do now that you have time to do it — travel, golf, playing with the grandchildren. You fill in the blanks.

If you are like most retirees, you will see the usefulness of creating and adhering to a budget. You want your money to work for you without significant risk, so you are careful not to overdo your spending. Your goal these days is to maintain your independence for as long as possible while continuing to live your life in the style and manner to which you have grown accustomed. It is during this phase that you will probably follow a strategy of income planning that involves a guaranteed income stream that you cannot outlive.

The time to begin thinking about this income stream is not when you need to turn it on, but during the accumulation phase of your life, when you are in what is called the "red zone" — 10 years or so away from your retirement date. The retirement income planning you do then will determine your comfort level in the distribution phase. For most folks, this means zooming in on critical answers to specific questions about the future. How much will you need to live on after you retire? What will your expenses be? What do you want to do with your free time? How much money will you need to do that? What about legacy? If that is important to you, the time to work that out will be when you are doing your retirement income planning.

Next is identifying all sources of income. How much will likely come from Social Security, and what is the best collection strategy to employ? How much will come from private investment accounts, such as pensions, savings, individual retirement accounts (IRAs) and simplified employee pensions (SEPs)? If you have a 401(k), what is your exit or withdrawal strategy, and how much can you expect to receive from it?

How Much Do I Need?

"How much do I need to have saved before I can retire?" There is no easy answer to that question. It is different for each one of us — just like our height, weight and shoe size. There is no one-size-fits-all solution. It must start with analysis.

Like most people, I dislike TV commercials. One caught my eye a few years ago, however. It was put out by a large insurance company and featured a man walking his dog down the street. He was carrying something huge and bulky under his right arm. It appeared to be a large orange number that had either been photoshopped into the video, or was a prop made from Styrofoam. The number was specific, too. Like $1,230,000, or something like that.

The man carrying the number encounters a neighbor on a ladder trimming his hedge. Sitting atop the hedge is the word "Gazillion," also orange and very large.

"What do you have there under your arm, Clark?" asks hedge trimmer.

"Oh, that's my number. It's what I figure I need to have saved before I retire," replies the dog walker. "Say, is that your number?"

He is referring, of course, to the word "Gazillion" sitting atop the hedge.

The hedge trimmer is embarrassed and stammers, "Yeah, gazillion, bazillion. I'm just going to throw something at it and hope for the best."

The point was well made. The dog-walker had done the due diligence to determine exactly how much he needed to save before he retired and was working toward that goal. The guy trimming his hedge had no clue. Which one would likely end up with a successful retirement? Obviously, the first fellow. Why? Because he had taken the time to get specific with where he was in the financial stream of time and knew exactly where he was going.

How big should your nest egg be for you to safely retire? Different strokes for different folks, but a good rule of thumb is 10 times your final annual salary.

The Times, They Are A-Changin'

"There's a battle outside and it's raging. It'll soon shake your windows and rattle your walls, for the times they are a'changing."
~ Bob Dylan, 1961

You may be a baby boomer if you remember the lyrics to early Bob Dylan tunes played on vinyl discs on turntables. Truth is, times have been changing for quite some time when it comes to sources of income in retirement.

It wasn't too long ago that financial planners referred to something called the three-legged stool of retirement:

- **Social Security**
- **Personal pension**
- **Personal savings**

So, what has changed? Lots.

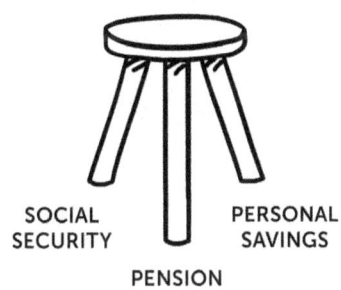

SOCIAL SECURITY   PERSONAL SAVINGS

PENSION

The Disappearing Pension

For one thing, pensions have gone the way of lava lamps and the rotary-dial telephone. Times were when you worked 40 or so years for a big company, and they gave you a gold watch and a lifetime income in the form of a good chunk of your salary. Did I say *guaranteed* **lifetime** *income?* Yes! But how many people do you know who are fortunate enough to retire on those terms today? If you are one of them, consider yourself very fortunate. You are part of an elite group, diminishing in number.

Why have company pensions become virtually extinct? It all started, believe it or not, with the Studebaker. As Jeff Foxworthy would say, "You just might be a baby boomer if you know what a *Studebaker* was."

The Studebaker Corporation, named after founder John M. Studebaker, started out making horse-drawn wagons and entered the automobile business with electric cars in 1902. Two years later, they introduced a gasoline-powered model. For those who *don't* remember them, Studebakers had a reputation for being fast, dependable and futuristic in design. One model in the late 1950s had three headlights — one on each fender and another, like a third eye, in the center of the grill. It was thought by many to be ahead of its time, which is perhaps one reason why it failed to survive. Whatever the reason, the 1960s were not kind to the Studebaker and the last one rolled off the line on March 16,1966.

When Studebaker began sending workers home with pink slips, they began to realize they had made pension promises they couldn't keep. Thousands of workers either got nothing or had their pension payouts cut drastically. They raised such a public outcry that Congress and the media took note. Legislators passed the Employee Retirement Income Security Act of 1974 (ERISA), to regulate pension plans.[10]

One byproduct of ERISA was the IRA (individual retirement account). In those days, you could contribute up to $1,500 per year into an IRA, reduce your taxable income by that amount, and save for retirement. Another product of this legislation was the 401(k). Companies could allow workers to contribute to a tax-deferred retirement plan. Contributions to 401(k) plans would reduce their income taxes and be invested in mutual funds, where they would grow tax-free until retirement, and then they would be taxed upon withdrawal.

Good old Uncle Sam! Of course, tax deferral, don't forget, is good for the government, too. Tax *deferred* is not tax *free.* The government forfeits a small slice of the tax pie now to get a much bigger slice later.

But back to pensions. Once government control became part of the pension picture, more and more companies began to back away from offering them. The penalties for backing out on their promises made it costly and prohibitive.

Fewer and fewer of my clients have defined-benefit pension plans. It seems they have been replaced these days by plans such as IRAs and 401(k)-type retirement savings programs, which are dependent on individual contributions. But these retirement savings plans are not the guaranteed lifetime incomes that pensions were. If they are invested in the stock market — and most of them are — they have a measure of risk. They can lose value in market downturns. In retirement, they last as long as the money you have invested in them lasts. They can also be tax "time bombs." While employees were glad to see their taxes reduced when they made

---

[10] Roger Lowenstein. The Wall Street Journal. Oct. 1, 2013. "The Long, Sorry Tale of Pension Promises." https://www.wsj.com/articles/the-long-sorry-tale-of-pension-promises-1379723751.

their contributions, once they retire and enter the distribution phase of their lives, they are taxed on withdrawals. The questions I am most frequently asked about tax-deferred retirement plans are how can I make my invested funds last throughout my lifetime, and how can I pass the money to my heirs without leaving them with an unreasonable tax burden.

What About Social Security

There is legitimate, widespread concern about the long-term viability of the second leg of the three-legged retirement stool — Social Security. Why is that? Primarily because the number of those receiving money from the Social Security program is increasing, while the number of those paying into the program is decreasing. That can't go on indefinitely. Unless Congress acts to fix it, the Social Security trust fund will run out of money by 2034, according to the 2016 Social Security and Medicare trustees annual report.

That means baby boomers are probably going to get what they expect from Social Security. Their children and their children's children, on the other hand, may not.[11]

What changes are lawmakers likely to make to fix Social Security? Several options are on the table as I write this. Among them are:[12]

- Reducing benefits for the wealthy
- Moving retirement age up from 66 to 68 or even 70.
- Cutting back on COLAs (cost-of-living adjustments)
- Increasing the payroll tax

[11] Jeanne Sahadi. CNN Money. June 22, 2016. "Social Security trust fund projected to run dry by 2034." http://money.cnn.com/2016/06/22/pf/social-security-medicare/index.html.

[12] Matthew Frankel. The Motley Fool. July 24, 2016. "Is the Social Security Trust Fund Running Out of Money?" https://www.fool.com/retirement/2016/07/24/is-the-social-security-trust-fund-running-out-of-m.aspx.

- Increasing the cap on Social Security taxable wages
- Removing the cap on Social Security taxable wages

The perception that Social Security is on the ropes and gasping for breath may be a bit overblown, but it is clear: Social Security is not the sturdy pillar of retirement planning it once was. Even the Social Security Administration acknowledges this in the following statement on 2017 Social Security statements:

"Social Security benefits are not intended to be your only source of income when you retire. On average, Social Security will replace about 40 percent of your annual pre-retirement earnings. You will need other savings, investments, pensions, or retirement accounts to live comfortably when you retire."

To view your Social Security statement online, all you have to do is create a "my Social Security" account. The website to go to is www.myaccount.socialsecurity.gov. In my line of work, I come across many documents produced by the government. I find many of them difficult to understand, and some downright undecipherable. But the statements produced by the Social Security Administration are written in plain English and are easy to understand. The site is interactive, easy to maneuver through and offers a world of information about your personal Social Security account. In the plethora of information presented on the website, the piece that is probably most important to people is how much they can expect to receive and when. That question is answered in remarkably clear detail.

Personal Savings

So, if pensions are an endangered species and Social Security is threatened, that leaves one leg of the three-legged retirement stool — personal savings. The truth is, many Americans just haven't saved enough for a carefree retirement. According to the Economic Policy Institute (EPI), the average American family has retirement savings of only $95,776. Averages don't paint the whole picture, of course. Some families have no savings whatsoever and are deeply in debt, while others have saved 10–20 percent of their earnings all their lives, but a savings shortfall clearly exists in America.

"The State of American Retirement," an EPI report published on March 3, 2016, blamed the widening retirement gap on the shift from traditional pensions to individual savings. When pensions were in vogue, workers were automatically enrolled. Employees are not required to contribute to 401(k)-type plans, so many of them don't. According to the EPI, participation in all employer-based retirement plans have declined since 2000.

Author's note: Press the pause button, please, dear reader. If you are in your accumulation years, and you work for an employer that offers matching funds on a 401(k) plan or its equivalent, by all means, participate. Not participating in a matching program, at least up to the match, is like refusing free money.

Another concern is how the quality of retirement can be threatened by an economic downturn, as the following paragraph from the above-mentioned EPI report observed:

> "Much of the 401(k)-era coincided with rising stock and housing prices that propped up family wealth, even as the savings rate declined. This house of cards collapsed in 2000 to 2001 and again in 2007 to 2009. In 2013 most families still had not recovered their losses from the financial crisis and Great Recession, let alone accumulated additional savings for retirement."

> "Recessions can be very damaging to workers nearing retirement," the report continued, "since they have less time to make up losses and their retirement outcomes are influenced more by investment returns than new contributions. In addition, many older workers who lose jobs tap retirement savings."

The report concludes, with Social Security benefit cuts looming, and pensions disappearing, children and grandchildren of baby boomers should be saving more, not less. Sadly, such is not the case.[13]

As we mentioned in the previous chapter, there is no set-in-stone answer to the question, "How much should I have in my nest egg before I can comfortably retire?" But if 10 times your annual salary is a good number to shoot at, then the sooner you can start saving toward that goal, the better.

If accumulating 10 times your final annual salary seems a bit unreachable, CNBC Senior Personal Finance Correspondent Sharon Epperson offers the following simple formula. Keep in mind, if invested wisely, your savings will be earning interest as you add your contributions.[14]

- In your 20s, put enough away so that by the time you turn 30, you'll have the equivalent of your salary saved.
- By 40, aim to have 3 times your salary saved up.
- By age 50, you should have enough saved to equal 6 times your salary.
- By age 60, your savings should be 8 times your salary.
- And 10 times your salary by the full retirement age of 67.

Why the 4 Percent Rule No Longer Works

Decades ago, financial planners were limited when it came to tools and strategies. All they had to work with were stock market and risk investments, or annuities with unacceptable options. Annuities back in the old days, for example, lacked flexibility. You could turn a sum of money into an income you couldn't outlive, but if you died a few months after the payout began, your heirs did

---

[13] Monique Morrissey. Economic Policy Institute. March 3, 2016. "The State of American Retirement." http://www.epi.org/publication/retirement-in-america/.

[14] Sharon Epperson. CNBC. Feb. 11, 2016. "What's the magic number for your retirement savings?" https://www.cnbc.com/2016/02/11/whats-the-magic-number-for-your-retirement-savings.html.

not receive the balance of the account. The insurance company kept the money. Those products weren't too popular with the baby boom generation, and who could blame them?

When it came to securities, many advisors believed in and advocated what they called the "4 Percent Withdrawal Rule." This was the notion that their retired clients could confidently withdraw 4 percent, adjusted for inflation, from their invested nest egg each year and never run out of money.

Where did they get that idea? It originated with William Bengen, a California financial planner who wrote the book, "Conserving Client Portfolios During Retirement." Bengen tinkered with the numbers, using various drawdown percentages, to see how a retirement account, invested in nothing but stock market securities, would fare over a 30-year period. His idea was to land on a percentage, adjust the amount withdrawn for inflation each year, rebalance the portfolio each year and make the money last for three decades. Four percent turned out to be the magic number.

Bengen's research was not necessarily flawed. It was true — at the time. But times have changed since the mid-1990s when he conducted his research. You remember the 1990s, don't you? That's when a circus monkey could pick stocks and come out a winner on Wall Street. Since Bengen's book came out, we have experienced the bursting of the tech bubble in 2000 and the financial crisis and ensuing Great Recession of 2008. The volatility of the market during what has been referred to as the "lost decade" of the 2000s has ushered in a new reality. Confident investors of the 1990s have been replaced by the wary investors in the new millennium who have seen a stock market characterized by steep drops and weaker-than-expected recoveries.

Simply put, the 4 Percent Rule, once considered the Holy Grail of investing, no longer works and has been kicked to the curb by all but a few die-hard financial advisors.

Some Things Never Change

While it is true that the scene of the financial world has changed and is continuing to change, one thing remains the same: People still want the same things out of their retirement. They want to enjoy it without having to spend sleepless nights pacing the floor worrying about money. In short, they need an adequate income they know they cannot outlive.

When I conduct seminars, I like to ask the question, "How much are you willing to lose from your portfolio at this juncture of your financial lives?" Most will answer zero, yet their portfolios are not positioned accordingly. What follows in this book are a few common mistakes people planning for retirement make and how to avoid them.

FIVE COMMON
RETIREMENT MISTAKES

Mistake No. 1: Investing as Though You're Still Working

You finally made it. You turned 65 and retired. The office staff threw you a great party, and the boss said some really nice things that got you all choked up. You cleaned out your desk, said farewell to the gang, and left the workaday corporate world in your rearview mirror.

But now, as you head into that vast unknown called retirement, you have a sinking feeling in the pit of your stomach. You wonder if your money will be enough to last the rest of your life. The last thing you want to do is run out of funds a decade or so later and have to go back to work. After all, you'd go back as what? A Walmart greeter or a french-fry specialist at a fast food place? You have tried to invest wisely, but now that you no longer have a paycheck rolling in, you are having to create your own paycheck from your savings and investments. You look at the price tags on items you purchase a bit longer than you used to. At restaurants, you tend to look at the right side of the menu a little more closely.

Financially speaking, you have passed a point of no return. When you were working, you had a positive cashflow. If your investments didn't pan out the way you had planned, you could always adjust the bottom line by postponing your retirement. But once you pull the retirement trigger, that option is no longer open to you. If you re-enter the workplace, you will likely have to start over. You shudder at the very prospect of that.

If you are like most retired folks, you look at investing through a more conservative lens than you did when you when you were working. The reason for this is simple. You loathe the idea of losing any significant portion of all you have built up throughout your working years because of a sudden stock market reversal.

Roller Coaster Rides

The stock market, with its many ups and downs, is often compared to a roller coaster ride. It's an apt comparison. The other day I saw a cartoon showing the cars of a roller coaster flying off the rails and hurtling off into thin air. On the front of the first car were the words, "Wall Street." In the cars were petrified investors with their arms flung out and mouths agape. In the front car, a wide-eyed fellow, obviously scared to death, is sitting beside a man who nonchalantly tells him as the car plunges earthward, "Don't panic. This is just a correction."

I don't know about you, but the older I get, the less enthused I am about climbing on one of those things. We have them here in North Carolina. Carowinds, an amusement park in Charlotte, North Carolina, boasts of several corkscrew rides. But perhaps the scariest of them all is the Fury 325. This Giga-Coaster (one with a drop of over 300-feet) is 6,600 feet long, and according to its publicity description, "climbs taller than the Statue of Liberty [305 feet], drops at a stomach-churning 81-degree angle and thrusts its riders around turns at 95 miles an hour."[15]

When I was younger, I enjoyed being jerked around by the relatively tame rides at the Rowan County fair when it came to town in the fall. But these days I prefer quieter pleasures—jogging on the beach down near Oak Island, or sipping a glass of iced tea at one of the casual restaurants by the Intracoastal Waterway down around Southport, North Carolina. I enjoy smooth and stable, not stormy and unpredictable.

It's a little like that with investing in retirement. You want your money to work for you, but you don't want to risk losing it all. When I meet with people who have left a job and still have their money in a 401(k) or a 403(b) plan, invested in stocks and

---

[15] NBC News. March 25, 2015. "Check Out Fury 325, One of the World's Tallest Roller Coasters." https://www.nbcnews.com/news/us-news/check-out-fury-325-americas-terrifying-new-roller-coaster-n330191.

mutual funds, I will usually ask them a series of questions to determine what they want their money to do for them. If the answers I get from them tell me that they are more interested in preserving their wealth than gambling with it, I will show them options allowing them to roll over their accounts into IRAs with more conservative investment choices.

What I find all too often, is people don't realize they are at a different place on the investing timeline.

"Treat your wealth like your health," says one axiom. When you were a youngster, it was altogether appropriate that your parents took you to a pediatrician for medical care. When you became an adult, however, did you keep your pediatrician as your primary care physician? No, you moved onto a different level of care that matched your physical growth. By the same token, you wouldn't seek advice from a general practitioner for a heart problem.

Likewise, your financial timeline should dictate how you invest. Seek advice from a financial counselor who is familiar with strategies that can help ensure your money lasts as long as you do.

Does that mean, now you are retired, you should put your money in a savings account at the bank, or in a CD, where it will earn a miniscule amount of interest? No. It's the *degree* of risk you should be thinking about.

An investing rule of thumb that has been around a long time is the "Rule of 100." The essence of it is this: Take your age and subtract it from 100, and that is the percentage of your assets you can place at risk. The rest should be invested where your principal is protected. Another way to calculate it is to simply place a percent after your age. That is the percentage of your assets that should be kept safe from risk.

CHAPTER FIVE

Mistake No. 2: Not Protecting Yourself From a Significant Financial Loss

In Chapter Two, we touched on losses and how they impact wealth. You don't have to have the biggest gains, if you can just avoid some of the bigger losses. One of the biggest mistakes retiring investors make is concentrating too much on gains, and not enough on preventing loss.

Which is better, to find $10 or not to lose $10? Wait a minute, Robert! Aren't they both one and the same? Not really. Ask any economic psychologist. They will tell you about something called "the endowment effect." Here's the definition from the financial terms website, www.investopedia.com:

*"**Endowment effect** – In behavioral finance, the endowment effect describes a circumstance in which an individual values something which they already own more than something which they do not yet own.*

Sometimes referred to as divestiture aversion, the perceived greater value occurs merely because the individual possesses the object in question. Investors, therefore, tend to stick with certain assets because of familiarity and comfort, even if they are inappropriate or become unprofitable. The endowment effect is an example of an emotional bias."

Interesting, eh? What is the old saying? "A bird in the hand is worth two in the bush?" An example of the endowment effect, according to Investopedia, is when people inherit shares of stock from deceased relatives and refuse to sell them, even if keeping them is outside their risk tolerance and does not match their investment goals.

To illustrate the endowment effect with his students, one economics professor gave a coffee mug with the university's logo on it to a few of his students. He didn't make too much of it — it was just a gift of a coffee mug. No big deal. A couple of days later, he held up one of the mugs and asked each student in the class to place a value on the mug, write it down on a folded sheet of paper, and hand it in. The students who had been given a mug placed a higher value on it than the ones who hadn't received one.[16]

When emotions and money mix, our ability to make good decisions suffers. During the 2008 market crash, I personally witnessed many investors who had all their assets invested in equities lose as much as half of their life's savings. CNBC Wall Street reporter John Carney puts the total figure of America's market losses during that financial crisis at $6.9 trillion. That's *trillion,* with a "T." I know million, billion and trillion all rhyme. It's easy to fail to grasp just how much that is. But a million seconds is 12 days. A billion seconds is 31 years. A trillion seconds is 31,688 years. A trillion dollars is so huge an amount that you only hear politicians

---

[16] Investopedia. "Endowment Effect."
https://www.investopedia.com/terms/e/endowment-effect.asp.

use it. Perhaps that is because they don't really have a concept of just how much they are talking about.[17]

There is no way that numbers can ever measure the personal agony experienced by those who saw decades of their life's savings go up in smoke. I saw the faces of some who attended my seminars the week after the Dow fell 777 points in one day. Sept. 28, 2008, recorded the largest single-day point drop in the history of Wall Street. It was also the day many who were hoping things would turn around and the market would right itself lost faith and had to realize Wall Street's wheels had come off.[18]

The expressions on faces I saw were a combination of shock and resignation. Many had followed the advice of their brokers who had used expressions like "stay the course," and "hold the fort," and "don't worry, it will bounce back." They uttered these expressions, of course, to keep their clients from pulling their assets out of their accounts and going to cash. But the idea did as much to ease their pain as a baby aspirin does for a migraine headache. These folks were heartbroken, and didn't know which way to turn or whom to trust.

I once had a client show me a citation he had received from a North Carolina State Trooper after his car had skidded into another car in one of the rare snow storms that visit the Piedmont area of the state. The charge? "Failure to act in the interest of safety." The man was irate.

"Failure to act in the interest of safety?" he said. "What does that even mean?"

I thought, but did not say, "It probably meant you should have stayed off the icy roads."

---

[17] Tysk News. "Million, Billion, Trillion." https://www.tysknews.com/Depts/Taxes/million.htm.

[18] Kimberly Amadeo. The Balance. Feb. 7, 2018. "Stock Market Crash of 2008." https://www.thebalance.com/stock-market-crash-of-2008-3305535.

While they may not have caused the 2008 financial debacle, those who lost huge sums of money during that period failed to act in the interest of safety.

21st Century Investing

Investing in the 21st century is much different than it was in the 20th century. The old buy-and-hold concept, for example, no longer works. The flaws in this approach became painfully manifest when the tech bubble burst in 2000. Many of the companies in which brokers were investing ended in "dot-com." When the tech bubble burst, many of those companies vanished like dandelion spores in a stiff breeze. When the market became exuberant beyond all logic and reason, instead of receding when the value of tech stocks dropped, the flow of money pouring into them actually *accelerated.* Investors just couldn't get it through their heads that the party was over.

Traditionally, buy-and-hold assumes, over long periods of time, the market will rise. In general, that assumption is correct. But the question investors must ask themselves is, do I have that much time? The question is: Do you have that much time?

"Why 'buy and hold' isn't all it's cracked up to be" is the title of an article written by Thomas Kee, President and CEO of Stock Traders Daily in January 2014. In it, he makes the point that buy-and-hold investors "who were fully invested in 2000, only became whole again in 2013."

So, if you are approaching retirement, how long do you have to recoup your losses in the next (and there will be a next) market crash?

Kee observes a proactive strategy is one that manages risk — one that will work during both the ups and downs of the stock market. But what often happens is people abandon proactive strategies when the market is on a roll.

"We cannot tell if the market will fall hard again," writes Kee, "but one thing is for sure: If the market falls, buy-and-hold investors will incur another setback."[19]

When Emotions Get in the Way

Portfolios need to be (a) flexible, and (b) managed by professionals who are not emotionally involved.

Do-it-yourself investing is like do-it-yourself surgery. Sure, you can do it. But it probably isn't a very smart thing to do.

Dialogue you will never hear at a dinner party:

"How did your knee replacement surgery go?

"Oh, great! I did it myself!"

You don't have to be a rocket scientist to know the success formula for all investing is to buy low and sell high. So, why is it that so many investors fail to pull that off? In a word — emotions.

As stock market volatility can take us on a roller coaster ride of finance, our emotions often take a ride, as well. Instead of taking a proactive — or even inactive — role in our finances, our sweaty-palmed emotional state can prompt us to be reactive, one of the worst kinds of approaches to our finances! The following illustration can give you an idea of how this sort of roller coaster of emotion plays out and affects our financial standing.

---

[19] Thomas H. Kee Jr. CNBC. Jan. 3, 2014. "Why 'buy and hold' isn't all it's cracked up to be." https://www.cnbc.com/2014/01/03/why-buy-and-hold-isnt-all-thatcommentary.html.

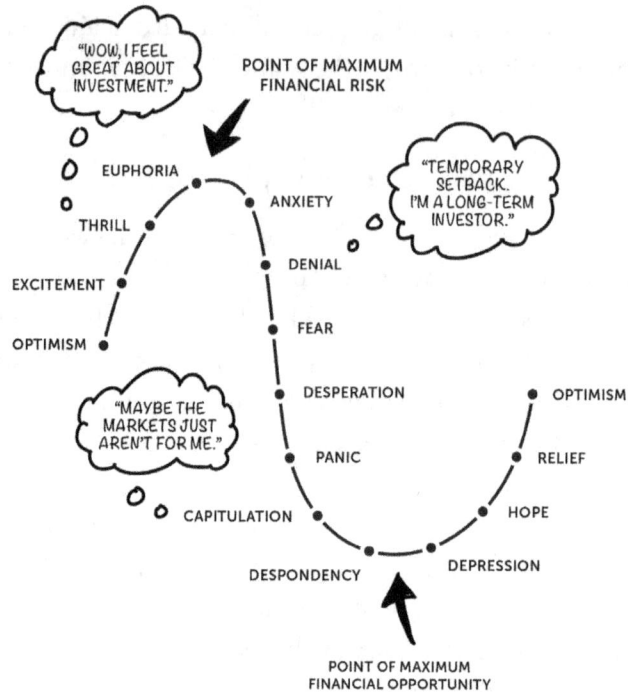

Optimism — I just took the plunge. I bought that stock I was following. I paid $75 per share for it. As soon as it hits $125, like all the analysts say it will, I will sell and take profits. I watch the ticker. The share price is steadily climbing. I am thrilled and excited! Another month goes by. The share price is steaming toward $120 per share. Investing is easy! Who knew Mama raised such a smart kid?

Anxiety — Oh no! Has there been a major shift in the alignment of the planets? The ticker at the bottom of the screen indicates this stock is starting to go the other way! I must stay glued to the TV and watch the financial channel. I must gaze endlessly at my smart phone, watching hour-by-hour for the slide to end. But it doesn't end! Now, it's all the way down to $60 per share!

Denial — This can't be happening. It won't continue. Sure, the stock we bought at $75 per share just hit $50, but this is a temporary setback, and I'm a long-term investor. Just a market hiccup, that's all.

Fear and Desperation — The slide is continuing. If I sell now, I have to admit that I have no investing super powers and can't time the market. But I can't let this go on. I have already lost way too much. I have to sell. Maybe I'm just not cut out for investing in the stock market anyway. I will try to learn a valuable lesson from all of this and get out now while there is still something to salvage.

Hope — I can't believe it! That stock I sold has climbed back up to $70 per share and the reports are all positive it will continue to climb. I was a fool to get out when I did. You know what this is? It's a buying opportunity! That's what it is! But I'm not sure. You know what they say, "Once bitten, twice shy."

Optimism — The stock has hit $80 per share! This is the signal I have been waiting for! I was right all along about this stock. I knew it all along. I'm jumping back in. With both feet, this time. No guts, no glory, right?

And the process starts all over again. As the chart illustrates, emotions affect our timing. We get in too late and get out too early. As I said at the beginning of this piece, treat your wealth the way you treat your health. Let an unbiased professional who is fully trained — not emotionally involved! — manage your portfolio.

Sleep — the Best Risk Test

A farmer who lived in the Midwest, out where the wind can kick up quite a storm at night, had gotten to the point where he couldn't do all the work himself on the farm. Harvest time was fast approaching, so he decided to advertise for a hired hand. He soon had several applicants. Each listed much the same qualifications: experience, strength, good work ethic. But one applicant added something unique. He told the farmer he could sleep on a windy night.

The farmer couldn't get it out of his mind. He told his wife about the applicant.

"That's what he said," the farmer told his wife. "I can sleep on a windy night."

"What does that mean?" his wife asked.

"I have no idea," the farmer said. "But I think I will hire him."

So, the farmer decided to hire this fellow, even though he couldn't find out exactly what "I can sleep on a windy night" meant.

As the weeks went by with the harvest in full swing, the hired hand was proving his worth. He worked hard and proved to be an asset to the farmer. His only failing was coming in late for supper most nights. But the farmer was still curious about the "sleep-on-a-windy-night" business.

One night a terrible storm broke loose over the plains. The wind howled, bending the trees over. The farmer went to wake the hired hand so they together could go to the barns and sheds and make sure that all on the farm was OK. But the hired hand couldn't be roused. The farmer finally shook him awake.

"Quickly, quickly!" he panted. "We must go out and tend to the animals in the storm!"

Blinking awake, the hired hand politely told the farmer there was no need for concern. He had seen the weather report. He had closed and bolted the doors on all the barns and sheds. He had given all the animals extra feed and had placed heavy tarpaulins over the hay bales and lashed them down with extra rope. There was nothing left to do.

With that, the hired hand fell back asleep. The farmer went out into the howling wind, and everything was just as the man had said. So, the farmer also went back to bed, happy in the knowledge his farm was safe. He was also pleased he had hired a farm hand who could sleep on a windy night.

The best gauge of how well your assets are invested within your risk tolerance is whether you can sleep peacefully when the last headline you read was, "Record Wall Street Crash!" Or, "Market Collapses."

I'm sure most of us have experienced sleepless nights when some family trouble or trauma strikes. At such times, we may pace the floor and wring our hands out of concern and worry. But, if we find ourselves having one of those sleepless nights because we are stressed out over our investments, then it's a sign we are way outside our comfort zone and our assets are not invested within our risk tolerance.

Like the hired hand who could sleep peacefully on a windy night, the time to make such preparations is not when the storm hits, but well before. A competent financial advisor will know this. A competent financial advisor will ask enough questions to ascertain just how much risk is too much for each client. Only then, after taking everything about the client into account — age, years to retirement, financial goals, etc. — will a competent financial advisor talk strategies. That way, when economic storm winds hit, you can sleep well at night, knowing your life's savings will not be threatened.

CHAPTER SIX

Mistake No. 3: Not Guaranteeing Your Basic Income Needs

As I told you in Chapter Two of this book, I'm not a big fan of TV commercials, but some of the catchier ones stick in your mind like Velcro, especially the ones that touch on financial planning. I saw one recently involving a large group of people of different ages and walks of life, gathered in a big field for an experiment. They were asked, "How much do you think you will need when you retire?" As you would expect, answers were all over the place.

"I don't know," shrugged one man who appeared to be in his early 40s. "Half a million dollars?"

"A million?" said a 60-ish woman with graying hair.

Each participant in the experiment was instructed to write their answer on one end of a yellow ribbon about 6 inches wide, and then walk with it from the center of the field until their ribbon ran out. Ages were marked in concentric circles that extended out from the center, and whatever age they stopped at was the age at which it was projected they would likely run out of money. Most people guessed too low, and ran out of money early.

One woman said, "It only got me to age 70. I'm going to have to re-think this thing!"

Another young man who had underestimated was comically trying to tug his ribbon past the 50-year-old mark.

What was the point? Just guessing at how much we need to save for retirement is a waste of time. It takes careful planning and working with a professional to get it right. Another point the commercial made is that we don't know how long our retirement will last. The age markers stopped at age 105!

There is another concept at work here. When you were working, you had a regular, steady paycheck you could count on to cover everyday expenses. Why wouldn't you want the same thing in retirement? And why wouldn't you want the peace of mind of knowing you could count on that paycheck for as long as your retirement lasts? In the informal surveys I take with people who are exploring their retirement options, most people say they would like to have a guaranteed lifetime income, but not many know that such a thing is possible, or how to make it happen. (Author's note: I suppose I should be relieved and grateful that this is the case. It gives me job security.)

Making It Happen

Coming up with a strategy that (a) fits your unique financial circumstances and goals, and (b) provides a guaranteed lifetime income you can't outlive that will adequately accommodate your lifestyle is not as easy as a finger snap. It requires thought, due diligence and the help of a professional.

It reminds me of playing a musical instrument. Ask nearly any-one who doesn't play a musical instrument if they would like to play one, and they will say yes. But few are willing to put forth the time and effort required to acquire the skill.

The same company that aired the above commercial came out with another equally catchy one in 2016. It also made a salient point about financial planning. The commercial's narrator invited six people into a room with six pianos and handed each of them a book, "How to Play the Piano in 5 Steps." None had ever played the piano before, of course. The camera shows them looking from their books to the keyboard, and painfully plunking out discordant notes. Then the narrator explains the point of the experiment. The piano novices didn't know it, but they only had 25 minutes to learn to play. Why 25 minutes? The narrator explains: "In a recent survey of workplace retirement plan participants, 75 percent said they spent 25 minutes or less making investment choices for their retirement."

When a horn sounds, the surprised piano students are told to close their books and audition. They all sound terrible, of course, except for one, who appears to be playing a Scott Joplin rag with easy precision. When the music continues after he removes his hands from the keys, you see it is a *player* piano. No hands needed.

The point of the one-minute spot is, just as learning to play the piano is complex and involved and requires a teacher, so, too, is planning for retirement. It is not something you want to approach cavalierly — not if you wish to get it right.

Why do so many people not have a plan for income when they retire? Is it because it is human nature to procrastinate? Is it be-cause people just don't like to think about the future if it presents any degree of complexity to them? I think so.

I was surprised when I saw a 2015 report aired by the financial TV channel, CNBC, claiming 34 percent of Americans have no financial plan at all. I thought it would have been higher! The report went on to say 58 percent of Americans thought the financial planning they had done was insufficient. Sadly, people spend more time planning the details of their summer vacations than they spend working out the details of what will replace their paychecks when they retire.[20]

Which brings us to the question, what will replace *your* paycheck? Pensions are a dying breed, and the Social Security blanket is too thin and too small to cover you adequately. That means, as the old axiom puts it, "If it is to be, it's up to me" to provide my own pension. But how?

One method is through using an annuity.

Ah! The "A" word that strikes fear and loathing into the hearts of many — *annuity!* If you are one of those folks who catapult themselves screaming across the room, frantically searching for two pieces of wood to put together in the shape of a cross to ward off evil spirits at the very mention of the word, please stay calm. It may not be what you think. But what is behind such thinking? Some people swear by annuities while others swear at them.

What's Behind Annuity Bias?

I don't think any single financial product or instrument is as polarizing and misunderstood as the annuity. Yet, American consumers tend to vote with their pocketbooks. If you go by the sales figures, a lot of people are putting their money into annuities. LIMRA, an insurance research organization, reports total sales of all annuities in the U.S. amounted to $222 billion in 2016, thanks

---

[20] Anna Robaton. CNBC. April 29, 2015. "Study: 33% of Americans have no financial plan." https://www.cnbc.com/2015/04/29/one-third-of-americans-lack-a-future-financial-plan-study.html.

in large measure to record sales of fixed index annuities, which totaled $60.9 billion in 2016.[21]

So, why the love 'em or hate 'em thing? Let's start at the beginning, shall we?

History of Annuities

It is the heyday of the Roman Empire. Roman soldiers are the highest paid, best trained, best fed and most well-equipped fighting men in the world. They have marched and conquered everywhere in the known world. But conquering other nations is a dangerous business; you could get killed out there. Some enterprising businessman in Rome got the bright idea to create a contract called an *annua* (Latin for yearly) and allowed soldiers to buy one. The "annua" promised to provide an annual stipend to a soldier's family if he fell in battle. The concept soon spread to Roman citizens. They could make a single payment to a money-lender who would, in turn, guarantee regular payments to them once they reached a certain age.

In 17th-century Europe, governments created *tontines* — contracts that promised future incomes based on the terms purchased now. They used the proceeds from these to fund their wars.

In America, in 1759, a company in Pennsylvania established a fund to benefit Presbyterian ministers and their families. The idea was for ministers to pay small amounts into the fund in exchange for the promise of lifetime payments when they quit the pulpit.

The first company to offer annuities to the public was The Pennsylvania Company for Insurance on Lives and Granting Annuities in 1812. Later, annuities were used during the Civil War by the United States to compensate Union soldiers. President

---

[21] LIMRA Secure Retirement Institute. Feb. 21, 2017. "Fourth Quarter U.S. Annuity Sales Survey." www.thinkadvisor.com/2017/02/21/fixed-annuity-sales-hit-record-1174-billion-in-2016.

Abraham Lincoln endorsed an annuity plan to help families of veterans with war-related disabilities.

In the 1930s, the modern concept of the annuity gained traction when the Great Depression caused people to turn to insurance companies as a haven for their cash when banks began failing and they had lost confidence in the stock market.[22]

From Simple to Complex

Automobiles have changed over the years, becoming sleeker and more powerful. They have also become more complex. It's a little like that with annuities. Adding bells and whistles to the original concept has made them do more, but it has also added to their complexity, as we shall see in this chapter.

Let me say here that I think this is where the misconceptions about annuities begins, especially in the media. I see some writers and reporters who probably couldn't answer five basic questions about annuities presume to pass judgment on them. Usually, it only takes me a couple of paragraphs to spot it when the writer of an article about annuities doesn't know what he or she is talking about. Instead of doing their homework, they pass along twice-told tales and add quotes by pundits who often know less than they do about the subject. So, let's dive into just what makes annuities tick.

Categories of Annuities

The term "annuity" is a broad one. Like the word automobile. Under that broad heading you have everything from tractor-trailer rigs to sports cars. Then, as a sub-category, there are Fords, Chevys, Lamborghinis and Toyotas. So, part of the confusion about annuities comes with lumping all of them into one category.

---

[22] Investopedia. "Introduction to Annuities: the History of Annuities." http://www.investopedia.com/university/annuities/#ixzz3waqZQsvc.

There are hundreds of annuities out there, some so dramatically different from the original they should be renamed.

Take *variable annuities* for example. They came along in 1952. A variable annuity is a stock market investment in an annuity wrapper. The idea of this annuity "mutation" is to allow mutual funds to grow tax-deferred. Not a bad idea, especially when the stock market is on a roll. When the market flourishes, you don't feel the pinch of fees and charges that go along with mutual funds, which is usually what variable annuities are invested in. But what happens if the market tanks? The VA can lose value.

One of the bells and whistles of the variable annuity concept is an insurance provision that allows investors to pass along the original amount invested to their heirs at death. Some investors mistake this for a guarantee of principal while living. It's not the same at all.

Variable annuities are usually sold by stockbrokers, while traditional fixed annuities are typically marketed by insurance agents. You can lose your principal in variable annuities. Your principal is protected in fixed annuities. This is a "nutshell" definition of the variable annuity, but you can see how far afield the concept has strayed from the traditional fixed annuity from which it sprang. Yet, they are both called "annuities."

So here is where "annuity bias" might originate: Uncle George and Aunt Mae have a few variable annuities in their brokerage account. All is fine until the stock market crashes, and they lose a bundle. Uncle George gets out his annuity statement and sees those ugly parentheses that indicate a loss. He is furious! This represents a good chunk of his life's savings. He tells Aunt Mae, "I will *never* buy another annuity as long as I live! They are *horrible!*"

Aunt Mae tells her sister, Juanita, who knows about as much about annuities as she does about nuclear fission. Juanita forms the opinion that all annuities are awful and horrible. She flinches when she even hears the word. Can you see things from her point of view? I can. As Benjamin Franklin said, "Someone convinced against his [or her] will is of the same opinion still." It shows how easy it is for us to form opinions about things we know little about.

There are a few financial concepts out there I go out of my way to warn folks about when they are approaching retirement. The variable annuity is one of them. I am not the only one. Apparently, Suze Orman is not a fan either. In her book, "The Road to Wealth," on page 510, she relates this question that was put to her at a seminar: "My financial advisor is recommending that I buy a variable annuity within my retirement account. What should I do?"

Her answer was straightforward. "Get another financial advisor," she replied.

With variable annuities, fees can range above 3 percent of your annual account value. [23]

So, let's say you have a 6.5 percent growth, and your VA costs 5.5 percent. Your return just shrunk to a paltry 1 percent! The reason VAs are so fee-heavy is because they have sub accounts similar to those of mutual funds. They also have administration fees, rider fees (if applicable), mortality fees (if applicable) and other charges.

Traditional Fixed Annuities

Having changed little over the years, traditional fixed annuities are boringly simple and straightforward. They are generally regarded as a reliable place to put money. Strictly from a growth perspective, annuities are often compared to a bank CD but with better interest rates. As I write this, traditional fixed annuities pay

---

[23] Dana Anspach. The Balance. Aug. 23, 2016. "Variable Annuity Fees—If They're Too High, Your Account Will Suffer." https://www.thebalance.com/variable-annuity-fees-to-ask-about-2389027.

around double what bank CDs do. Traditional fixed annuities promise lifetime income payouts for either a set period or life.

Typically, you get a 10 percent free withdrawal per year, but you will pay a penalty if you take out more than that before the surrender charge period expires. Penalties for early withdrawal usually start around 10 percent and decline until the end of the surrender period, which is usually between seven and 10 years.

That's a thumbnail sketch. What's the downside? When you opt to receive a payout from a traditional fixed annuity, you must "annuitize" the contract. If you die prematurely, let's say two months after annuitizing, and you have chosen the "life" annuity payment option, your beneficiaries don't get the balance of any unused portion of the account value. As far as the insurance company is concerned, they have fulfilled their part of the contract by making payments for the lifetime of the annuitant (you) and the case is closed. I'm not a big fan of that deal, either.

The Fixed Annuity "Makeover"

In the mid-1990s, when the stock market knew only one direction — up — some actuaries in the insurance industry responsible for product design must have done some brainstorming that went something like this:

Actuary One: "Wonder what would happen if we took the safety of the traditional fixed annuity and combined it with the growth potential of the stock market?"

Actuary Two: "Yeah! And what if we eliminated that part where you had to annuitize your contract to get a lifetime income?"

Actuary Three: "Yeah, that way, the heirs could get the unused portion of the account when the annuitant dies!"

Actuary One: (gets excited and spills coffee) "And instead of having a fixed interest rate, we could make it so the upward movement of the stock market dictated the interest earnings!"

Actuary Three: "Hey, and what if we made it so that, when the market goes up, your account value goes up, but when the market goes down, you don't lose?"

Maybe such a conversation never actually occurred, but the insurance industry did come up with that very product in the mid-1990s. Keep in mind, I have given you just a brief overview. There are several moving parts to it, many more than I have described in detail here. But you have the essence of it.

The product has gone by several names, too — hybrid annuity, equity-indexed annuity, income annuity. But the one the insurance industry prefers to use is *fixed index annuity,* or FIA. To understand this better, let's take the name apart one word at a time:

- **FIXED** — It is a fixed (not a variable) annuity, and the investor's money is not at risk in the stock market, so it keeps the safety attributes of the traditional fixed annuity. The annuity is backed by the insurance company and its claims-paying capacity. The annuitant owns a contract with the insurance carrier that spells out the income provisions.

- **INDEX** — The annuity's rate of interest is determined by the performance of a stock market index, like the S&P 500, the Dow Jones, the NASDAQ, or a combination of these or others without your money ever being invested in the market. When the index value goes up, so does your account value, usually up to a cap (or sometimes reduced by a spread). For example, if the index is up 20 percent, and your cap is 5 percent, you will get only 5 percent interest that year.

- **ANNUITY** — Despite the bells and whistles, it's still an annuity. It has an accumulation phase (the time during which your money grows), and an annuitization phase (when you receive monthly payments from the annuity). Interest credits are tax-deferred, but you will pay taxes when you withdraw the money. Other typical annuity features apply. Surrender charge periods are usually around 10 to 12 years with declining surrender charges until the 10 to 12 years expire, and then there are none. While you are in deferral, you are typically allowed to withdraw 10 percent of the value from the contract annually without paying surrender penalties. Some FIAs allow for larger distributions than 10 percent if the owner is confined to a nursing home or is terminally ill. There is no penalty imposed for any size withdrawal once the contract has passed the surrender period. Depending on the type of contract you have, you may also pay an additional 10 percent tax penalty on withdrawals prior to age 59 ½.

Income Riders

Many FIAs are purchased with an **income rider** attached. As the term suggests, they are optional. On average, they cost around 1 percent of the annuity value per year. To illustrate how the income rider works, think of a motorcycle and a sidecar. The motorcycle is the annuity and the sidecar is the income rider. The motorcycle can function independently of the sidecar, but the sidecar is useless without the motorcycle.

Income riders go by several names, depending on the insurance company:

GLWB—Guaranteed Lifetime Withdrawal Benefit

GLIR—Guaranteed Lifetime Income Rider

GLIB—Guaranteed Lifetime Income Benefit

These riders provide an enhanced guaranteed lifetime income, the amount of which is based on a formula set by the insurance company. As income generators, these riders work differently than the old-style traditional fixed annuities. With traditional fixed annuities, once you started lifetime income, that was it. If you died six months later, your beneficiary got nothing.

Please know also not all income riders are alike. Their terms and conditions vary from company to company. But they all do essentially the same thing — provide a guaranteed lifetime income stream.

As I said at the beginning of this chapter, they have more moving parts than their predecessors. Because the income rider has its own "machinery," it's easy to confuse it with the base annuity. They are *not* the same! Think of one account with two ledgers. Ledger one is the **base account.** That's the account you may withdraw 10 percent from per year without penalty until your surrender charge period ends. That's the amount you can access in a lump sum. Then there is the **income account,** which cannot be accessed as a lump sum, and whose sole purpose is to provide you with income payments — sort of like a pension — over time. The income account is used as a calculation base for income. That's all it does.

Moving Parts

Is your head starting to hurt? I told you it was a little complex. But I felt it was important to introduce you to these products because they are one solution to the real and pertinent problem of securing a guaranteed income in retirement. They are not for everyone, but they have their place in the overall income planning picture and, for some, they are the missing puzzle piece.

When I am face to face with clients, I use software that not only illustrates the function of the FIA, but uses data from their own financial situation. You see it much more clearly when *your* numbers are plugged into the equation.

CHAPTER SEVEN

Mistake No. 4: Not Paying Attention to Your Portfolio Costs

Not too long ago, a good-natured couple came into my office looking for advice. The man told me they were both retired.

"Well, *he* is retired," the wife clarified with a laugh. "My occupation is listed as a 'homemaker,' and I work as hard as I always did!"

They told me their story.

He had worked for a local company for approximately 30 years, and had built up a little over $300,000 in his 401(k). Upon his retirement, the couple had gone to a local bank where, upon the advice of the banker, they had rolled over his 401(k) to an IRA and invested it in a variable annuity.

The wife pulled out a handful of papers from a brown folder and handed them to me.

"Can you tell me what this is for?" she said, pointing at some figures she had underlined on the variable annuity statement. "Can this be right?"

The couple had deposited a little over $300,000 into the account and they were paying just over $11,000 in fees.

"Yes, those figures represent the total fees you are paying each year for the privilege of being in this investment," I explained.

She shook her head slowly and her expression darkened.

"I remember asking the person at the bank what were the fees for this account. They told us the fees would be no more than they would be on any other investment," she said.

"I think we were lied to," her husband said.

These stories are not rare. When I show people what they are paying in fees on some investments, they are shocked and find it hard to believe. This pair was not rich. This was a large portion of their life's savings — money they intended to use to make ends meet in their golden years. It was difficult for them to imagine their money lasting long in retirement if they had to pay $11,000 a year in fees in addition to taking money from these funds to pay their expenses.

Beware the Fine Print

How do you say, "read the fine print" in Latin? I think it's "caveat emptor," or something like that, which I'm sure someone probably shouted in ancient Rome when they had just gotten ripped off by a street vendor. The phrase, when translated, means "buyer beware."

When I travel, I like to stay at nice hotels with clean rooms, comfortable beds with expensive mattresses and thick sheets. I like thick, fluffy towels and real bars of soap that fit in your hands, not those little slivers that are wrapped up so there is more paper than soap. I want the TV to be one of those new, high-definition flat-screen jobs that hangs on the wall, not an antique boxy thing. I want there to be a business center and a gym, even if I don't always use them.

It depends on which city you stay in, of course, but the average four-star hotel room will cost you about $200 per night or more. I am not naïve enough to think "nice" doesn't come at a price. And I am perfectly willing to pay extra for comfort and convenience. But what I *do* resent is the feeling that I am being tricked or taken advantage of.

Case in point: Recently I went online and made a reservation at a four-star hotel in a major city. They advertised a rate of $228 per night on their website, which seemed par for the course. But when I went to check out, the total was over $300! Why? Hidden fees such as:

- Resort fee - $65
- Garage parking fee - $20
- Bottled water - $4.50
- Internet - $15

You know those "complimentary" bottles of water they put in your hotel room? The ones you could buy downstairs in the gift shop for $1.50? They will cost you three times as much if you crack the top off one in your room. And it may be just my opinion, but internet should be free of charge *everywhere,* like air.

Where did I learn about these hidden charges? At the checkout counter, not the website. Don't get me wrong. It's not just the money; it's the principle of the thing. I felt like the victim of unfair trade practices.

Even our local supermarkets are reprehensible. According to a 2014 article in the Boston Globe, it could be as simple as a 1-pound can of coffee that only contains 11 ounces. Or the container that used to be a ½ gallon of ice cream that is now 1 ½ quart — but, surprise, it still costs the same! Yogurt containers that once held 16 ounces look the same from the outside, but check the underside. That little hollow space just shortchanged you two ounces. You must read the small print on the packaging to find out.[24]

The point is, hidden fees are everywhere — *including your investments!*

What Happened to Transparency?

I will never forget the day a 67-year-old woman came to our office for a free consultation. She was a retired teacher. She had a brokerage account containing several hundred thousand dollars. She handed me a copy of her most recent statement and said with a disdainful tone, "I'm an educated person, but I can't understand this statement!"

Her complaint is not an unusual one.

Her visit to our office took place shortly after the 2008 market crash. We did a line-by-line explanation of her statement for her. Not only had she lost over 35 percent of the value of her account, but her assets were 85 percent at risk — highly inappropriate for someone of her age group.

The line-item examination of her statement revealed something else that troubled her. In addition to her losses, she was also paying painful percentages of her balance in unwanted fees and hidden charges.

Brokerage Account Fees

Is it any secret that big brokerage companies charge commissions? No. In fact, they publish broker commission comparison tables. But the ones I looked at weren't very transparent. There was so much fine print and so many asterisks it was easy to get

---

[24] Jane Dornbusch. Boston Globe. Feb. 11, 2014. "Increasing food prices spark trend of package downsizing." https://www.bostonglobe.com/lifestyle/food-dining/2014/02/11/the-incredible-shrinking-package/Ti6VwQCCcg0whLdr8bHnyJ/story.html.

lost. I doubt if the ordinary investor would try to understand these charts and tables.

Imagine sitting down at a table in a café for lunch, looking the menu over and deciding on a salad. Price of salad — $5. But wait, there's an asterisk, which leads you to some tiny print at the bottom of the menu. Come to find out, there are extra charges for lettuce shredding, tomato slicing and carrot grating. Then, there is another asterisk. There's the waiter's delivery fee. Your $5 salad ends up costing you $14!

When you compare broker commission tables, you find they each try to brand themselves as a low-cost provider. Company A charges $8 per trade and Company B charges $14. If you don't read the fine print, you may conclude that Company A charges less. But then you find out Company A charges extra to discuss the transaction with an agent. You have to read the fine print to discover some brokerages charge an "inactivity fee" if you leave the account idle too long. Others may charge you to open the account or deposit money into it.

The thing about fees in investment accounts and 401(k) accounts is you don't notice them when the stock market is on an upswing and your account is making money. Like submerged rocks at the shore, you don't notice them until the tide goes out. Hidden fees surface most glaringly during market downturns.

Let's say you inherit $100,000 and pay 5 percent for a retail, or "A-share," mutual fund account. The conversation between you and a broker may go something like this:

YOU — "I've just inherited this sum of money and I want you to invest it for me."

BROKER — What would you like for me to invest in?"

YOU — "You're the expert. Just use your best judgment and make some money with it."

Don't laugh. Many investors have told me of just such conversations.

So, the broker puts it in an "A-share" mutual fund account and charges you 5 percent. A month goes by, and your first statement arrives. It will reflect the broker's commission, which is $5,000. To make the math simple, assume the market is going sideways at the time, and there are no losses and no gains. Your balance is $95,000. But that's not the end of the story. Mutual fund fees range anywhere from 1–3 percent.

Here's a paragraph from the United States Securities and Exchange Commission website under the heading: "Calculating Mutual Fund Fees and Expenses:"

> "Fees and expenses are an important consideration in selecting a mutual fund because these charges lower your returns. Many investors find it helpful to compare the fees and expenses of different mutual funds before they invest."

Here's another note of caution from the SEC:[25]

> "A mutual fund's fees and expenses may be more important than you realize. Advertisements, rankings, and ratings often emphasize how well a fund has performed in the past. But studies show that the future is often different. This year's 'number one' fund can easily become next year's below average fund."

Hidden Fees in 401(k) Plans

I am convinced there are many American workers who don't realize they are paying any fees at all on their tax-deferred retirement savings plans, such as 401(k)s and 403(b)s. That is probably why a law was passed in 2012 requiring 401(k) plan administrators to disclose full details of all such fees to employees. Perhaps now more workers realize what a big bite these hidden fees can take

---

[25] U.S. Securities and Exchange Commission. Aug. 10, 2010. "Calculating Mutual Fund Fees and Expenses." https://www.sec.gov/reportspubs/investor-publications/investortoolsmfccmfcc-inthtm.html.

from their life's savings they have socked away in these retirement plans.

A 2016 survey found 67 percent of Americans didn't know they paid fees for their 401(k)s. They would no doubt be surprised to learn that there are record-keeping fees, administrative fees and charges by various names that come off the top before any of their gains or contributions ever reach their assets.[26]

It may surprise others to learn that 401(k)s employ middle men, or third-party managers, who receive "revenue sharing" (also known as kickbacks) from the mutual fund companies.

Ross Kenneth Urken of AOL Daily Finance conducted a revealing interview with Robyn Credico, senior consultant at Towers Watson, a large New York-based human resources consulting firm in 2012, in which Credico said, "Sometimes those investment companies say to the record-keeper, 'I'll give you a little bit of the investment to offset your record keeping fees.'" That "little bit" of the investment translates into hundreds of thousands of dollars diverted from the accounts of workers.[27]

The Government Steps In

Hidden fees and unnecessary charges on investment accounts rob the American investor of money they could be earning in their accounts. When people find out about them, they naturally wonder where the government is in all of this, and what happened to regulation. Things are improving in that regard. The Wall Street crowd may not like it, but more and more full-disclosure legislation is showing up. Rules encouraging all stock brokers to become

---

[26] CNBC. Feb. 14, 2017. "Hidden 401(k) fees can destroy your retirement dreams." https://www.cnbc.com/2017/02/14/hidden-401k-fees-can-destroy-your-retirement-dreams.html.

[27] Ross Kenneth Urken. AOL.com. June 25, 2012. "401(k) Fees: What You're About to Learn Will Shock You." https://www.aol.com/2012/06/25/401k-fees-disclosure-rules-action/.

fiduciaries (putting their customer's interests above their own) are gaining traction. Fiduciaries are required to disclose all fees charged the investor at inception of the advisor/client relationship.

Hidden Costs in Mutual Funds

Most mutual fund investors are familiar with expense ratios. But one of the most open secrets of mutual fund companies is that, due to the nature of mutual funds and trading within the funds themselves, there are costs that are never disclosed in any prospectus or featured in any expense ratio. Even if those costs are only 1 or 2 percent, that can have a significant impact over time.

In case you are wondering what an extra percent or two can mean to retired people, think about one couple I know who enjoys traveling. They have small camper and love visiting national parks, but they do not consider themselves wealthy and they budget carefully. If they have a portfolio of $500,000 in mutual funds and pay 2–3 percent in fees, that's $20,000 to $30,000 per year. When you put it in terms of dollars and cents instead of percentages, it is easy to see how much of their hard-earned money falls through the cracks. What if an independent fiduciary advisor could reduce those fees by half? That would give this retired couple an extra $10,000 to $15,000 in traveling money each year. Do you think that would make their lives more comfortable and help them enjoy their retirement more? Absolutely! Or, they could apply the savings back into their investments. I'm sure they could find many uses for that kind of money.

The Impact of Investing Fees

Suppose you have an investment portfolio getting a 7 percent annual rate of return, but you are paying 3 percent in fees. You are only netting a 4 percent return. Now, put yourself in the position of someone who is in their 60s striving to reach a retirement goal. How many extra years will you have to work to get there?

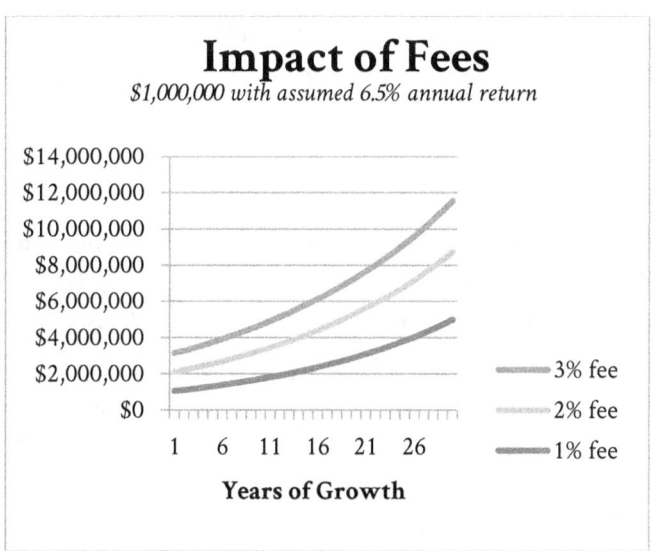

Impact of Fees
$1,000,000 with assumed 6.5% annual return

Years of Growth

Vanguard Group founder John "Jack" Bogle, commenting on the impact of investing fees, said "Costs are a crucial part of the equation."

In a Public Broadcasting System special that aired in April 2013, Bogle said, "It doesn't take a genius to know the bigger the profit of the management company, the smaller the profit investors get. The money managers always want more and that seems natural for most businesses, but it's not right for this business."

Over a 50-year period, even small fees can add up and consume as much as one-third of your portfolio, Bogle points out. "What happens in the fund business is that magic of compound returns is overwhelmed by the tyranny of compounding costs," he adds.

Bogle continued with this dire warning: "It's a mathematical fact. There's no getting around it. But the fact that we don't look at it (is) too bad for us. ... If you want to gamble with your retirement money, all I can say is 'be my guest.' But be aware of the mathematical reality... It has been proven right year after year after year. It can't be proven wrong. It's a mathematical certainty."

By the way, Bogle has quite a following in the investment world. They call themselves "Bogleheads®" and their mission is to point out unreasonable investment expenses and what they see as deceptive practices by Wall Street institutions.[28]

Front-End Loads

Here's another "gotcha" you may experience when moving out of one fund and into another. If you sell your current fund, you could owe a "back-end load," and there could be a commission (front-end load) when you buy the replacement fund. These are not necessarily "blind spots" as much as they are "hard-to-see spots." Why? Because they are probably in the prospectus. But did you read it carefully? Probably not.

Then there are capital gains taxes. If the fund you are selling has gained value since you purchased it, then you may owe capital gains taxes.

As an example of the effect loads can have on your returns, suppose you put $50,000 into a mutual fund and you were charged a 5 percent load. That's $2,500 right off the top that won't be working for you. That's a real killer when you calculate how much that costs you year after year in compound interest.

Morningstar Ratings

Morningstar is a Chicago-based investment research organization that rates mutual funds. Their ratings are objective. They aren't trying to sell you anything. They base their ratings on a mathematical evaluation of the fund's past performance and they

---

[28] Jason M. Breslow. PBS Frontline. April 23, 2013. "John Bogle: The "Train Wreck" Awaiting American Retirement." https://www.pbs.org/wgbh/frontline/article/john-bogle-the-train-wreck-awaiting-american-retirement/.

are quick to let their subscribers know their ratings are not a buy or sell recommendation. They rate funds like hotels — one to five stars, with five being the best. Their ratings adjust for risk and all sales charges.

The good news is investors are seeing a decline in mutual fund expense ratios since 2000. But, as mentioned earlier, there is more to consider than just the expense ratio. There are transaction costs.[29]

Transaction Costs

Because transaction costs don't appear as a line item on the prospectus, they can be hard to spot. Mutual fund companies are required to provide a "statement of additional information" to investors, but only upon request and, even then, because of the complex nature of these trading costs, the way one company reports them will likely be much different than another

What exactly are transaction costs?

When mutual fund managers buy and sell stocks within the fund, shares are traded (bought and sold). Those are transactions. Each time it happens, commissions are generated for the broker.

The SEC requires three years of brokerage costs to be disclosed in a fund's "statement of additional information," but the information is usually expressed in dollars. That means you must do the math to get the full picture of what these trades cost you. The rest of the cost comes from (a) bid-ask spreads, and (b) market impact costs.

Bid-ask spreads represent the difference between the highest price a buyer is willing to pay for a stock and the lowest price at

---

[29] Patricia Oey. Morningstar. May 23, 2017. "U.S. Fund Fee Study—Average Fund Fees Paid by Investors Continued to Decline in 2016."
https://corporate1.morningstar.com/ResearchLibrary/article/810041/us-fund-fee-study--average-fund-fees-paid-by-investors-continued-to-decline-in-2016.

which a seller is willing to sell. If a security has an ask price of $96 and a bid price of $100, the $4 in between will go to the broker of the sale. Again, this happens at the level of the individual stock within the mutual fund, so it isn't a cost you can expect to see in a fund prospectus, but, especially for mutual funds with high turnover, it can still be a significant cost to a mutual fund owner.

Market-impact costs are the cost to the mutual fund of trading at inopportune times in the market. This sometimes is because of the mutual fund itself — if a large mutual fund with lots of shares in XYZ company trades those shares, the shares could in turn decrease in value precisely because a large mutual fund is selling its position. Because that mutual fund is so large and is trading such a large volume, the XYZ company shares could even decrease in value *before the mutual fund has finished the transaction,* meaning the fund could lose money on the sale.

So, why don't mutual fund companies automatically figure these costs into their return projections? Because every dollar of cost reported offsets the gains picture. If investors don't know the costs of a mutual fund, they can't determine where the performance bar needs to be set. You can't accurately measure the depth of a stream if you can't find the bottom. Likewise, undisclosed costs make the fund's performance reporting inaccurate.

CHAPTER EIGHT

Mistake No. 5: Not Knowing How Much Money You Need in Retirement

You may be a baby boomer if you remember watching the old black-and-white episodes of Rod Serling's "The Twilight Zone" back in the early 1960s. If you are a bit younger, maybe you have seen re-runs. For some reason, every Fourth of July, the SyFy cable channel runs a "Twilight Zone" marathon for 24 hours.

In one classic episode, some bad guys steal a truck hauling a million dollars in gold bars. One of the gang is a scientist who has figured out a way to put the thieves in suspended animation for 100 years. The idea is, by the time they wake up a century later, the heat will be off and they can spend their ill-gotten gains in leisure. They park the truck in a mountain cave and crawl into their capsules. One of the criminals plots to wake up early and take all the gold for himself. The only problem is, in the world he wakes up in, gold has no value! While he slept, people discovered a way to make synthetic gold out of more plentiful metals, and it was no longer precious.

How ironic! When you stop to think about it, money is no more than paper or metal or, in some cases, numbers on a computer screen or an account statement. It is the value *assigned* to it that gives it worth. Even then, if you have lots and lots of money, but you can't get your hands on it, its present value to you is zero, isn't it?

The term for access to assets is "liquidity."

Cash is liquid. Real estate is not. Money in the bank is liquid. An asset that cannot be exchanged for cash easily without taking a loss is illiquid.

Illiquid wealth reminds me of the line from "Rime of the Ancient Mariner" by English Poet Samuel Taylor Coleridge: "Water, water everywhere, nor any drop to drink." But how much liquidity do you need in retirement? That's a good question, and the answer will be different for each individual. Lifestyles vary. To some, travel means going to the beach. To others, it means living in Europe six months out of the year.

Do You Have an Emergency Fund?

One of the cornerstones of intelligent financial planning is an emergency fund. How much do you need? Again, it varies. My blanket recommendation is to have at least six months' worth of living expenses socked away in a CD or money market account in case of some unforeseen emergency. Life is unpredictable. A natural disaster could strike. You could lose your job. Your car or roof could suddenly need replacing. Emergency funds need to be instantly accessible. You should be able to stroke a check for the funds or obtain them at an ATM. Think in terms of evacuation. It's in the middle of the night and you have to leave town *NOW!*

You grab some emergency supplies, clothes and *money* to get you through the emergency. How difficult will it be to obtain the cash?

As I said earlier, I recommend having at least six months' worth of income, or living expenses, at your immediate disposal. Nine months is even better.

Pick Any Two

Liquid assets have notoriously low rates of return. Remember when checking accounts paid interest? Well, you can still get interest-bearing checking accounts, but, as I write this, you are lucky to find a rate of even 1 percent. Even then, watch for high minimum balances, fees and service charges.

Sometimes just for grins, I like to poll audiences at my seminars and ask them to describe the *perfect* investment. I will sometimes write their responses on a whiteboard with a dry-erase marker, or on a flip chart. I consistently hear the same responses to the ideal investment:

- High returns
- Completely safe
- Highly liquid
- Completely tax-free
- Completely transferrable

The result of my ad hoc research is this: *The perfect investment doesn't exist!*

If I knew of an investment that would yield consistently high returns with no risk whatsoever, where you could access your cash instantly with the stroke of a pen or the push of a button, it would be criminal of me not to put all my clients in it. The truth is, investing comes with tradeoffs. Always has, always will.

In the early 1980s, I remember seeing a sign posted above the cash register at a small, locally owned hardware store in rural Rowan County, North Carolina, that caught my attention. I suppose it was the store owner's way of answering questions about why his prices were higher than prices at the mega-stores that were starting to invade the area. It read:

Great Service
High Quality
Low Prices
Pick Any Two!

Similar tradeoffs exist in the world of investing, too.

Take bank CDs, for example. They have the attributes of safety and tend to be more liquid (with the exception of some with early withdrawal penalties), but do not have high returns. Equity investments have the potential for high returns, but they come with varying degrees of risk, and you must sell shares at the going rate to turn the stock into cash. Fixed and fixed index annuities are safe from market risk because of the layers of downside protection provided by the insurance carrier and government regulations, but to realize their earnings potential, years of growth must transpire, and there are penalties for early withdrawal. So, you trade liquidity for safety and future growth potential.

Investing your money in retirement is a balancing act. You must weigh your options based on what is most important to you. Some who wait too long to save for retirement make the mistake of trying to play "catch-up" with risky investments. I love the quote attributed to Great Depression-era humorist Will Rogers: "I am more concerned about the return *of* my money than the return *on* my money." That should resonate more with retirees than those in their working years. During the accumulation phase of your life, you have time to make up losses. When you retire, time is not on your side, and "doubling down" Las Vegas style just isn't a good idea.

On the other side of the spectrum are those who play it too conservatively by putting every cent into fully liquid investments with no risk whatsoever. That may scratch your liquidity and safety itch, but is it the wisest use of your resources? Not for most of us. I call it the "Scrooge McDuck syndrome." You remember the Disney cartoon character Donald Duck's rich uncle? He was fond of romping in a room filled with cash. The idea of a duck frolicking in a room full of coins and bills was absurd, of course, but that was what made it humorous. Having all your assets where you can access them at a moment's notice may give you a warm and fuzzy feeling, but, with the exception of the emergency account mentioned before, idle assets equal poor financial management. Assets that are completely liquid are not working for you and will not keep pace with even a mild rate of inflation.

Occasionally, I see an article in the news where someone buried cash in jars in the back yard, or secreted it behind plaster walls in old houses only to have it discovered years later. In 2006, a Cleveland, Ohio, contractor remodeling a bathroom in an 83-year-old home near Lake Erie tore out a wall and found two metal boxes packed with $182,000 in cash from the 1930s. A wealthy businessman had seen one too many banks fail in the Great Depression and decided to put his assets where they would be accessible and safe. The stash was eventually divided among his 21 descendants.[30]

How Much Do You Need?

How much will you need in liquid funds when you retire? Pose that question to a room with 100 people and you will have 100 different answers. Why? Because each individual is different, and every financial situation is different.

---

[30] Associated Press. MSNBC. Nov. 8, 2008. "Cash found in house's walls becomes nightmare." http://www.nbcnews.com/id/27608773/ns/us_news-life/t/cash-found-houses-walls-becomes-nightmare/#.Wow7P5M-feR.

For example, if you are collecting Social Security *and* you are fortunate enough to have a generous pension, then you may be all set when it comes to income. Liquidity will probably not be a concern for you. Of course, once again, here is where lifestyle comes into play. Most people who come to see me tell me they want to travel more in retirement. I always ask them to define travel. For some, it means a trip to Myrtle Beach, South Carolina a couple of times a year. For others, it means touring the Holy Land and seeing the Great Wall of China. You get the idea. Different strokes for different folks in this area can translate into thousands of dollars. But if we don't answer those types of questions, I can't help clients figure out how much liquidity they need. I always tell clients to have more liquidity than they think they need.

CHAPTER NINE

Life Insurance as a Retirement Income Tool

Oops! I just said, "life insurance!" Please don't slam the book shut. It's not what you think.

When you say those two words, "life insurance," people get shivers of repulsion. No. 1, it's something they associate with death and dying, which no one wants to think about. No. 2, the stereotype that goes along with life insurance salespeople is deeply imbedded in our consciousness. If you ever saw the 1993 Bill Murray classic, "Groundhog Day," you can never forget Ned Ryerson, the obnoxious insurance salesman that Murray's character, weatherman Phil Conners, meets on the street day after never-ending day after finding himself in a time-loop of Feb. 2 in Gobbler's Nob, Pennsylvania. At first, Murray's character is polite. Then, as the plot progresses and he has to hear the same pushy come-on day after day, Murray finally decks Ryerson with a right cross, knocking the cheesy salesman out cold. Naturally, the audience claps and cheers.

History of Life Insurance

To fully understand why I would bring up life insurance as a possible tool for retirement income, let's go back to the beginning of the concept itself, to about 100 years B.C. when the ancient Romans ruled the world. As we covered earlier, Roman soldiers were well paid, but they worried about what would happen to their families if they fell in battle. They also had a superstition that, if they weren't buried with their ancestors, they would be tortured in the afterlife. Fighting Huns and Barbarians was a dangerous thing, but most of them came back alive. Just as the annua began in response to covering soldiers' families' income, as we covered in Chapter Six, some clever Roman solder got a clever idea of forming a burial club. They would all pay a small amount of money to belong to this club. Then, if they died in battle, they could be given a proper burial, and their families could be cared for. The concept of creating a risk pool to offset costs was born.

The burial club idea soon was adopted by ordinary citizens of the empire. They didn't call it life insurance, but as years passed, it became a business that produced profits for the organizers and administrators of the clubs and benefits for the members. The idea faded out with the fall of ancient Rome in 476 A.D.[31]

The concept of life insurance was reborn in 1662 when John Graunt, an enterprising Englishman, came up with the first life expectancy tables. He crunched the numbers on how long the average person would live in those days. Now that human mortality could be calculated to a reasonable degree, companies began offering contracts to people along the lines of the old Roman burial clubs. The term "underwriter" originated because the risk-taker would write his name at the bottom of a document that promised to pay a sum of money if the person named in the document died

---

[31] M Gillies. My Sendoff. December 2011. "Death Insurance Throughout the Ages." https://mysendoff.com/2011/12/death-insurance-throughout-the-ages/.

within a certain period. Factory work was dangerous, and people still remembered the deaths caused by the Black Plague, so it became a popular idea.

In America, the first organization to offer life insurance was the Presbyterian church. They formed an organization in 1759 to pay a sum of money to the families of ministers in the case of their untimely death. The idea was soon adopted by other churches. By 1837, there were more than 20 profit-making insurance companies operating in the United States.[32]

A Retirement Income Tool? Really?

Did I just hear you say, "OK, Robert, thanks for the history lesson, but how could life insurance be used to fund retirement?"

Good question. The concept of insurance is much more involved and complex than it was decades ago. Sure, the basic idea is to pay your family when you die. Like the old Hank Williams song said, "I'll never get out of this world alive." So, there's that. If you ask most Americans to tell you what life insurance is for, they will likely say, "to protect your family when you die." That is still the primary reason to purchase life insurance, but there is much more to it than that.

Again, a little history first.

There are two types of insurance — term and permanent (whole) life. As the name suggests, term covers you for a specified period, such as 10 to 30 years. Premiums for term life are lower than those for whole life, and for good reason. When the term is over, your insurance stops, and there is no refund of premiums. Whole, or permanent, life insurance has a contract feature that term doesn't have — cash value. It is this element of life insurance that makes it a potential retirement income tool.

---

[32] Think Advisor. Sept. 9, 2013. "A Brief History of Life Insurance." http://www.thinkadvisor.com/2013/09/09/a-brief-history-of-life-insurance.

The insurance industry went through a revolution of sorts in the early 1980s. The interest rates offered on the cash value component of whole life policies were low — around 1–2 percent. When interest rates soared to double digits in the late 1970s, insurance companies had to redesign their policies to compete with banks. Policies weren't transparent in those days, either. Policyholders were cashing in their permanent insurance policies and replacing them with much cheaper term policies and putting their cash in savings accounts for cash growth. The "buy-term-and-invest-the-difference" approach to life insurance soon came into vogue.

Seeing this, insurance product design people came up with a new approach — *universal life (UL) insurance.* This was permanent life insurance, but with many changes. First, it was transparent. All fees, charges and mortality costs were spelled out in the policy. Secondly, the cash value feature was made adjustable. Most policies of that era tied interest earnings to United States Treasury bills, or "T-bills," which were also returning double digits for a brief period during that era of high inflation. These new UL policies also allowed for flexible premium payments. Let's say the policyholder was the owner of a business. And let's say that business had a good year. That business owner could pump additional funds into his policy.

Wait a minute, Robert! Why would anyone want to pay *more* than the proscribed premiums for a life insurance policy? For the *interest earnings potential!*

Another feature of these new UL policies allowed policyholders to make withdrawals from their cash value in the form of low-interest loans. As long as they followed the rules of the policy, they could, in essence, become their own banker. If, for example, they needed to buy a new car, they could borrow the money from their insurance policy and pay themselves back, with interest.

Traditional retirement accounts mandated you had to be a certain age before you could withdraw your money or else you would pay a penalty. Not so with life insurance. Another edge these new policies had over traditional retirement accounts was tax advantages. By law, life insurance proceeds are paid income-tax-free to beneficiaries. What happens if you die owning a retirement account? You just created a taxable event for your heirs.

Indexed Universal Life Appears

And yea, it came to pass that the insurance industry said, "Let universal life insurance come to pass," and it was good. For a while, UL was the best thing since sliced bread and vanilla ice cream. Customers were returning to the insurance fold in droves. But when interest rates began to return to normal in the late 1980s, UL began to lose some of its luster. The stock market began to surge in the 1990s, and money began to flow into equities.

One thing about the free enterprise system? It hates a vacuum. Insurance companies had to re-tool once again — this time with something called indexed universal life (IUL) — formerly equity indexed universal life. This new IUL afforded policyholders the ability to receive interest credits based on the performance of a stock market index without ever actually investing in the market. When the market is up in any given year, your policy is credited interest based on the market gains, subject to a cap or participation rate that will limit your earnings. In years when the market is down, you don't receive any interest but you also don't lose any previously credited interest. This type of interest-crediting strategy is known as an "annual reset."

There was a time when investors could pump as much as they wanted into a universal life policy. No more. In 1982, the TEFRA, DEFRA and TAMRA laws were enacted to prevent the tax advantages of life insurance from abuse. TEFRA stands for *Tax, Eq-*

uity, Fiscal and Responsibility Act of 1982. DEFRA stands for *Deficit Reduction Act of 1984* and TAMRA stands for *Technical and Miscellaneous Revenue Act of 1988*. Together, they outline how a life insurance contract can be funded. Violation of these funding guidelines can cause your universal life insurance contract to become a modified-endowment contract (MEC) and it will lose all the tax benefits associated with life insurance. Nonetheless, an IUL policy can accumulate significant amounts of cash value while still keeping the tax advantages of a life insurance policy.

Among the frequently asked questions about using IULs is, "How safe are they?" After all, they are not insured by the FDIC, like money in the bank. No insurance product is insured by the FDIC; rather, they are backed by the financial strength of the issuing insurance company. Insurance companies are required by law to cover at least 100 percent of their liabilities with reserves. The government regulates the percentage of an insurance company's assets that can be held in certain assets, which has helped produce an overall record of remarkable safety and solvency. Life insurance and annuities, in fact, are the only vehicles that can guarantee principal protection while offering minimum growth guarantees for the life of the contract.

Well, folks, that's a broad-brush explanation of IUL. Whether you are a candidate for this type of insurance for income planning depends on your health (it is still life insurance, and there is some underwriting), your age and your financial objectives. But the following are some appealing attributes of having IUL as a potential source of income in retirement:

No loss of interest. The market crash of 2008 is still fresh in the minds of many baby boomers. Eliminating the possibility of losing money when market returns are negative is huge. The interest earnings built up by market advances are not affected by negative swings. Instead of limits on how much you can contribute each year, like many retirement plans, you are limited only by the size of your policy.

The possibility of higher than average interest. While safety is generally synonymous with low returns in the investment world, if the stock market index that your IUL uses to credit interest does well over the period measured, you could see some attractive interest earnings. The money grows tax-deferred, which is that much more of your money at work for you. Unlike qualified plans and annuities, the death benefits and cash values are transferred income-tax-free to your beneficiaries. Cash value life insurance generally bypasses probate since it is contractually private and involves no public records.

Tax-free cash flow in retirement. With IRAs and 401(k)s, you will pay taxes on what you withdraw. IUL rules can allow for a tax-free retirement cash flow using contract loans, which can provide you with a tax-free income in retirement. The strategy involves taking withdrawals up to the cost basis, then borrowing the remainder, as long as you keep the policy in-force. Please note that policy loans and withdrawals will reduce available cash values and death benefits.

The death benefit. Don't forget, even though you may be using it for cash growth and retirement income, a tax-free death benefit is there to protect your family in the event of your death. The death benefit could replace a lost pension or Social Security income for a spouse at your death. Some IUL contracts offer a disability waiver of premium rider that will pay premiums for you if you become disabled.

Some Precautions

IUL is not for everyone. As we have said often in this book, every individual is unique. There is no one-size-fits-all in retirement planning. These factors need to be considered when exploring IUL as an option:

- **It's a long-term commitment.** An IUL should be purchased primarily for the reason of providing a death benefit to your beneficiaries, which makes this a long-term financial product. The cash value of an IUL will be well below the premiums paid for the first 7 years or so. If you don't intend to keep an IUL for 10 to 15 years, don't buy one. It takes about that long for compounding interest to take effect on the cash growth side of things. The mortality costs and the fees for this type of policy are paid up front. Don't buy an IUL if you are going to cancel the policy shortly after you purchase it.

- **There are mortality charges involved.** This is true of any insurance policy, and IUL is no exception. So, don't be shocked when you see them deducted from the contract value. Naturally, these charges will offset some of the interest crediting in the account and reduce the net return. If the insured has health issues, or is a smoker, mortality charges may eat too far into the cash growth and make buying an IUL not a viable option.

- **Companies can change rates and fees.** Most carriers that offer IULs will provide the potential buyer with illustrations to project interest earnings in one column and fees and charges in the others. Historically, these rates and charges have been slow to change, but changes can be made from year to year by these carriers in order to remain profitable. In the wording of the policy, the company reserves the right to raise mortality charges if necessary, or lower caps on gains.

- **Too many unpaid loans from the policy could cause the policy to lapse**. If that occurs, the policyholder can be taxed on the sum of the cash taken out of the contract, less the premiums that were originally paid. Most carriers put provisions in place to prevent that from happening.

- **Moving parts.** As you can probably see by now, IUL insurance has more than a few moving parts. It reminds me of automobiles these days. Much more complex than those of yesteryear, but there's also much more under the hood. You need to know how the machinery of these products functions before you purchase, and that may require that you spend some time with someone who understands them and can explain them to your satisfaction. [33, 34]

---

[33] Justin Kuepper. Investopedia. Jan. 24, 2016. "Pros and Cons of Indexed Universal Life Insurance." https://www.investopedia.com/articles/personal-finance/012416/pros-and-cons-indexed-universal-life-insurance.asp.

[34] Jordan H. Smith. ThinkAdvisor. Aug. 19, 2017. Indexed Universal Life: It's Just a Great Investment." http://www.thinkadvisor.com/2017/08/19/indexed-universal-life-its-just-a-great-investment.

CHAPTER TEN

In-Service Rollovers: The 401(k) "Escape Hatch"

What is an in-service rollover and why would I want to use it?

An in-service rollover is an option most employees have if they are 59 ½ or older. It allows them to rollover all or a part of their 401(k) into an IRA. They can do this while they are still working and contributing to their 401(k), and the employer will continue to match if they are currently doing so.

Why would a person want to do an in-service rollover? There can be several reasons, maybe the 401(k) has high fees and poor investment options. Maybe the employee wants to make part of their money safer as they approach retirement.

Let me give you an example. Bob and Mary have worked for many years building up their 401(k)s. Both Bob and Mary are both 60 years old and plan on retiring in two to three years. Now, let's pretend that the year is 2006, and they plan on retiring in 2008 or 2009. As you may recall, we had a market correction of 37 percent in 2008, which would coincide with their retirement. How would this have affected their retirement plans? Disastrously! They most likely would have been forced to continue working until they were able to recoup enough of their losses to support their lifestyle without a paycheck.

OK, so when is the next correction, Robert? Well, needless to say, I don't know. If I knew, it would be the height of inconsideration not to tell you, wouldn't it? No one knows which direction the stock market will take even tomorrow, much less when the next big crash will occur. But could it coincide with the year you have chosen to retire? Absolutely! So, unless you would like to tack on a few extra years to your workaday routine, it would be a good idea to hedge your bets, right? That's where in-service rollovers come in.

What Are the Rules?

Meet John Doe. He is 60 years old. He is not ready to retire from his job at Mega Corporation. Not yet, anyway. He wants to wait until he is 65. But he has done pretty well climbing the corporate ladder, and just rolled nearly $800,000 of his 401(k) into an individual retirement account, or IRA, through an in-service distribution.

Why would Mr. Doe want to do this? Because he (a) feels his plan is charging too much in fees, (b) thinks it is investing in some underperforming funds, and (c) he wants more control of his retirement savings. Mr. Doe felt being charged 2 percent for domestic equity mutual funds that were mediocre at best was "highway robbery."

"Every dollar I pay in fees is that much I will not have in my pocket when I retire," he said. And he's right! His strategy is to roll a big chunk of his 401(k) into a no-load IRA company and "cut out the middle-man."

Some employees may have funds with acceptable performance levels, but they just want more choices. One way to achieve that goal is to move assets into an IRA where you can call the investment shots.

Did someone just say, "I've never heard of in-service transfers?" That doesn't surprise me. Laws governing qualified retirement plans allow employees who are 59 ½ years old (and even some who are younger) to roll over funds in their 401(k) plans while they are (a) still working and (b) still contributing to the plan. But most employers don't advertise this fact. Also, even though it is lawful, that doesn't mean the company you work for will allow you to do it — although the Profit Sharing Council of America estimates 77 percent of 401(k)s allow for in-service withdrawals.[35]

It is important to remember anyone who chooses to withdraw their money and spend the cash before 59 ½ will owe an extra 10 percent penalty on the taxable amount. The same penalty would apply to an employee who took a loan from a 401(k), then changed jobs and did not repay the loan.

There are rules, yes, and this option is certainly not right for everyone. But it can be a better way to manage your retirement assets if it fits your individual situation.

What About a Roth?

Simply put, a Roth IRA is taxed upfront but is tax-free on the back end. Like anything that touches Uncle Sam's tax eyeball, it comes with restrictions and conditions, but it can be a good strategy for those who want to get their tax obligations over and done with and not pay taxes in the future.

The idea was the brainchild of the late Senator William Roth of Delaware. He and Senator Bob Packwood proposed a bill in 1989 that would allow individuals to invest up to $2,000 with taxed money, but the earnings would grow tax-free and be with-

---

[35] Joseph Hogue. 401kRollover.com. March 24, 2016. "What is an In-service 401K Rollover?" https://www.401krollover.com/what-is-in-service-401k-rollover-plan/.

drawn tax-free at retirement. Congress established The Taxpayer Relief Act of 1997, and the Roth IRA came with it.

The Roth IRA is designed for working people, not for the wealthy. If you make too much money, you can't contribute to a Roth. The rules are a bit complicated, but as of 2018, if you are married filing jointly and earn more than $199,000, it's a no-go for the Roth. Couples earning between $189,000 and $199,000 can contribute on a sliding scale.[36]

Some of the advantages of Roth IRAs are as follows:

- You can withdraw your principal from a Roth IRA penalty-free and tax-free at any time. After 5 years, you can withdraw earnings if you are over 59 ½.

- Distributions from a Roth IRA do not increase your adjusted gross income (AGI) like traditional IRA distributions.

- You can contribute to a Roth IRA even if you also participate in a 401(k) or other qualified retirement plan.

- Contributions to a Roth IRA are taxed at today's tax rates with no "look-backs" for Uncle Sam if tax rates go up in the future.

- You can leave assets in a Roth IRA to your heirs.

- There are no required minimum distributions (RMDs) with Roth IRAs. However, beneficiaries who inherit Roth IRAs are subject to minimum distribution rules.

- If the account holder does not need the money and wants to leave it to their heirs, a Roth can be an effective way to accumulate tax-free income.

- Qualified Roth distributions do not affect the calculation of taxable Social Security benefits (see Internal Revenue Code Section 86(b) (2) (B)).

---

[36] Roth IRA. 2018. "Roth IRA Rules." https://www.rothira.com/roth-ira-rules.

What About Conversions?

Why would you want to convert your traditional IRA to a Roth? If you said, "to minimize taxes in retirement," go to the head of the class. Of course! Who wouldn't be attracted to a tax-free income? And, yes, the government does allow such conversions. But make no mistake — you *will* pay taxes on the balance you are converting that has not already been taxed. While there are income limits that apply to making Roth IRA contributions, there are no income limits regarding *conversions.* The rules for doing a Roth IRA conversion are a bit complex, so I recommend working with a professional to see it through properly. In a nutshell, there are three ways to do it:

The 60-Day Rollover. With this method, you have the proceeds from your traditional IRA made out to you personally and then roll the funds over into a Roth IRA account. It is *imperative* that you roll the funds over within 60 days, or you will be hit with a whopping tax bill (the full amount minus nondeductible contributions).

Trustee-to-Trustee Transfer. This method eliminates the possibility that the funds from your traditional IRA account will become taxable. Just instruct the trustee of your traditional IRA to direct the funds to the trustee of your Roth IRA. Some paperwork may be required, but it shouldn't be too much to handle and it is all done automatically.

Same-Trustee Transfer. This works well if you can set up the Roth IRA with the same trustee holding your traditional IRA. The funds are simply transferred from one account to the other.

Converting a traditional IRA or qualified plan assets to a Roth IRA is a taxable event and could result in additional impacts on your personal tax situation, including a need for additional tax withholding or estimated tax payments, the loss of certain tax deductions and credits, and higher taxes on Social Security benefits and Medicare premiums. Please consult with a qualified tax advisor before making any decisions regarding your IRA. It is generally preferable that you have funds to pay the taxes due upon conversion from funds outside of your IRA or qualified plan. If you elect to take a distribution from your IRA or qualified plan to pay the conversion taxes, please keep in mind the potential consequences, such as an assessment of product-surrender charges or additional IRS penalties for premature distributions.

High Earners Go for Roth IRAs

In 2010, when the IRS removed the income limit on Roth conversions, high-income earners began lining up to take advantage of the change. According to a January 2013 IRS statistics report, the new rules led to an 800 percent increase in the number of Roth conversions, representing a transfer of $64.8 billion. It was "the first time conversions exceeded contributions," the report said, adding 57 percent of the conversions were from people with six-figure incomes.[37]

A concept known as "the backdoor Roth" may be one way to avoid a big tax bill when you earn more than the income limit for a Roth, according to personal finance expert M.P. Dunleavy. This strategy involves funding a traditional IRA, then converting it into a Roth. As I write this, there are no income limits. That could change, of course. And you must be careful to follow the rules, but for now it is perfectly legal.

"When you contribute to a nondeductible IRA, you're effectively depositing after-tax dollars, so you'd only owe tax on the earnings when you withdraw (or convert). If you convert to the

---

[37] IRS. Jan. 3, 2014. "Fall 2013 Statistics of Income Bulletin Now Available." https://www.irs.gov/newsroom/fall-2013-statistics-of-income-bulletin-now-available.

Roth soon after, any earnings, and therefore taxes, are likely to be minimal," says Dunleavy.[38]

As this is not an investing textbook, nor is it a how-to manual on Roth conversions, I have only given you a thumbnail sketch here. Such strategies are not for everyone, and the regulations and rules are myriad and can be confusing. My best advice is to seek the help of a professional and understand the landscape thoroughly before moving forward.

---

[38] M.P. Dunleavy. Betterment. April 17, 2014. "Roth IRA Rules: Smart Ways to Avoid Taxes on a Conversion."
https://www.betterment.com/resources/retirement/401ks-and-iras/roth-ira-rules-smart-ways-to-avoid-taxes-on-a-conversion/.

CHAPTER ELEVEN

Money Zones: Red Money, Green Money and Hybrid Zone

R ed Money? Green Money? Isn't all money green? What are you talking about, Robert?

Assigning color to our assets is a simple way to visualize "safe" versus "at-risk" money. In most cases, investments fall into these two categories:

- **Green Money** — Safe financial vehicles. You know what you have and what you will see in the way of returns.
- **Red Money** — At-risk investments. You hope you get a good return, but it's not guaranteed.

You might say that *green* money is "I know" money, and red money is "I hope" money.

Dave and Cheryl came into my office for a consultation one Monday morning. They would eventually become clients, but at our initial meeting, we were interviewing each other to see if it was a good fit. I have found most people, when they are facing retirement, don't like losing money; once they begin to see the pool of assets they have accrued to this point will have to last them the rest of their lives, they become more conservative in their view. This was the case with Dave and Cheryl. They were very well-educated people — Dave an engineer and Cheryl a college professor.

At our first meeting, I did most of the listening while they did most of the talking. I wanted to know about their goals and what kind of lifestyle they envisioned for themselves in retirement. They told me they both wanted to travel. He was a history buff who loved visiting old battlefields and museums. She had a passion for photography and wanted to tour the Holy Land. They were also madly in love with their two granddaughters and planned on spending as much time with as possible on their "little ranch," as they called it, which consisted of a few animals they called their "petting zoo."

At our second meeting, after we decided to work together, we got down to the numbers. It was important to find out where they were on their financial journey, and where they wanted to be. They had done an admirable job of saving, and they had lived within if not below their means. For the most part, their documents were in good order. Dave and Cheryl were intelligent professionals, but when it came to investing, they acknowledged they were not the savviest people on the planet. As I was conveying to them how I might position their assets to help them work toward their retirement goals without running out of money, I could tell there was a bit of a disconnect. I wasn't getting through. That's when I got the idea to use the illustration of a traffic light.

"**Green money** represents safe money," I told them. "These are your assets that come with a defined rate of interest or return."

"Like CDs." Dave said.

"Yes, like CDs, money market or savings accounts," I said. "We use green money to take care of living expenses, like food, clothing, shelter, transportation — that kind of thing."

"**Red money**, on the other hand, is money you have invested at some degree of risk," I explained. "How much red money you have in your financial picture depends on your risk tolerance and how much green money you have set aside as a safety net."

In Dave and Cheryl's case, we were able to achieve a good balance of red money and green money. They understood their red money needed about a 10-year time horizon to be effective within the parameters of their risk tolerance.

"I get it," Cheryl said. "With the risk comes a greater growth potential, but since we don't know exactly how the red money will perform, we have to be more cautious the older we get."

I agreed. "That's where rebalancing comes in. We shift more from red money to green money as we age and get deeper into our retirement years."

The reason we call *green money* in a portfolio the "I know" money is because we know it will be there unless we spend it. It is safe and not subject to downside market risk. We know how green money vehicles will behave. Green money vehicles are usually in one of the following:

- Checking
- Savings
- Treasuries
- Fixed annuities
- Money market accounts

Since this money is not subject to downside market risk, the return on this money will be limited. But, they often have guarantees built in. And, in certain circumstances, that's just what we want for a portion of our portfolio.

The reason we call red money in our portfolio the "I hope" money is because we don't know what the outcome of the investment will be. We *hope* it yields a profit and we will not lose it, but we have no guarantees. Red money is typically invested in:

- Stocks
- Bonds
- Variable annuities
- Mutual funds
- REITS (real estate investment trusts)

These instruments are at risk of losing money because of market downturns or interest rate fluctuations. These "red money" investments carry all the upside potential of the market, but also all the downside potential. Traditionally, red money has more liquidity options than green money.

What About Yellow?

Yellow is the third color of the traffic light. It is between red and green. In traffic situations, it can either mean speed up or slow down, depending on how cautious you are as a driver. But for our purposes, it well illustrates "hybrid" products that combine the attributes of safety with the element of growth potential. Money in this zone often combines some of the features of our green money (safety and guarantees) with the features of our red money (upside potential and liquidity).

To take advantage of this, many of my clients choose to use a portion of their green money and a portion of their red money and combine it into this "hybrid" zone. How much is an individual choice, one which often comes back to the formula we discussed in Chapter Four — the "Rule of 100." This is an age-old investing rule of thumb that involves subtracting your age from 100 and viewing the result as the percentage of your assets you should place at risk. The rest should be socked away in the green-money zone where you can't lose it to market volatility.

Fixed index annuities are an example of a financial vehicle that combines safety of principal with growth potential linked to the performance of the stock market. Remember, FIAs are fixed annuities that credit interest to the underlying contract value based on the percentage change in a market index like the S&P 500 without actually putting the contract principal at risk in the market. According to an Insured Retirement Institute report, "FIAs continue to post strong sales as both a fixed income substitute — meaning a bond-like return without interest rate risk — and on the attractiveness of optional guaranteed lifetime income benefits."

One reason for the surge in these insurance products is the decline in traditional pension plans. The IRI reported that in 1985, "there were 114,000 private-sector defined-benefit pension plans, but by 2013 there were only 23,769 of these plans remaining, according to the Pension Benefit Guaranty Corporation (PBGC). The October 2016 Bureau of Labor Statistics' National Compensation Survey reports that only about 18 percent of private-sector workers have access to a traditional pension."[39]

Conclusion: For most American workers, if you want a guaranteed lifetime income, you will have to make arrangements for it yourself. Pensions are disappearing and Social Security is nice to have, but not enough to live on.

Balance and Diversity

The farmer's 10-year-old daughter wanted to help with the family chores.

"You can help your mother by gathering eggs from the hen house," her father told her, and handed her two small baskets lined with cloth. Excitedly, the young girl skipped down to the hen house to gather eggs. She found 12 eggs, which filled one of the baskets to the brim. Her job finished, she began skipping back up the path to the house. On the way, however, she tripped and fell,

---

[39] Insured Retirement Institute. December 2016. "State of the Insured Retirement Industry: 2016 Review & 2017 Outlook." https://www.myirionline.org/docs/default-source/research/iri-state-of-the-insured-retirement-industry---2016-review-and-2017-outlook.pdf?sfvrsn=2.

dropping both the empty basket and the one full of eggs. All of the eggs were broken in the fall. Moral of the story: *Don't put all your eggs in one basket.*

The same is true with investing. Balance and diversity are the keys to prudent investing during your retirement years. The smart thing to do is use a mixture of all the investment and financial vehicles mentioned in the preceding paragraphs, putting them to work in your portfolio according to the diversification formula appropriate to accommodate (a) your age, (b) your risk tolerance and (c) your financial objectives. Use all these vehicles to work for you. Spread it out in the right proportion.

There is a difference between *true* diversification and *perceived* diversification.

"Oh, I am fully diversified," said one fellow. "I have three financial advisors!"

That's not diversification, that's confusion!

Nor is diversification having your money spread out in different financial institutions. Nor is diversification having all your money invested in different versions of similar investments.

One client told me when he inherited a large sum of money from his uncle's estate, he knew he had to invest it somewhere, but needed advice.

"I looked up the word 'invest' in the phone directory, and contacted the first company I saw in the Yellow Pages," he said. "It was a big glass and steel building, so I figured they must know what they were doing."

The person assigned to help him invest his money showed him a pie chart with small cap stocks, large cap stocks, international stocks and mutual funds, and advised him to spread his money equally among the all of them.

"That makes you *diversified*," the stockbroker told him.

No, it didn't. His "eggs" were just in different areas of the same investment "basket," which he would soon learn when the stock market experienced a major correction.

True diversification is having multiple asset classes that hedge your risk and, in so doing, provide more dependable returns. Not all asset classes go up at the same time and down at the time.

Think of a farmer planting with the goal of feeding his family all-year round. What does he plant. All corn? All wheat? No, he plants multiple crops, crops that will produce harvests all-year round. He may also add some livestock to the mix, and work at preserving some of the vegetables and meat for the winter months. It's the same with your investments. It's good to take inventory of what you have working for you.

Correlation and Asset Classes

Correlation is the relationship between two investments. The essence of diversification is to arrange your holdings so they experience opposite price movement. If one asset class is beset by stagnation or decline, other asset classes either rise in value or at least hold their own. Having asset classes with identical correlation means that when one crashes, they all crash. There is a difference between asset classes and market sectors. Market sectors, for example, are manufacturing, technology and finance. Asset classes are fixed income, equities and real estate. The variety in asset classes can offset economic swings, while market sectors don't necessarily do that. No one knows what the stock market will do from one day to the next, but asset classes telegraph their movements. If we study market movements, we generally know how a certain asset class will react when the market moves up or down.

For example, some bond exposure in your portfolio may offer a hedge against equity exposure. If there is a pilot strike and all the airplanes are grounded, then rail and automobile travel is bound to increase, along with all the economic commodities associated with those sectors. Real estate investment trusts (REITs) might be good options to offset a fall in the value of equities. Emerging market bonds will perform poorly if the issuing country's main export falls.

Call it the yin and yang of investing. The idea is to stay truly diversified so you don't get caught by a market crash in your retirement years when you are spending nonrenewable resources.

Balancing Act

The key in all of this, from an investing perspective, anyway, is to keep things in balance. If you are a baby boomer, you probably grew up watching the old black-and-white variety show put on by Ed Sullivan every Sunday night on the family TV set. If you do, then you may remember Erich Brenn. If you don't remember him by name, you may remember what he did. He is the guy who would start plates spinning on poles and end up with as many as 12 of them spinning, each of them rotating on the tip of a 4-foot stick. While this was going on, Brenn would perform a juggling act in the background. Then one or two of the plates would lose their momentum and start to wobble. Brenn kept juggling. You wanted to scream at him, "That plate's going to fall!" But of course that was part of the act. Just when the plate was about to topple off the stick and onto the floor, he would jiggle the pole and get the plate going again.

Successful investing requires that same kind of awareness, timing and balance. As a professional, I see too many investors concentrating on short-range results and immediate return on investments instead of long-term investing for an income source in their retirement years. A balanced portfolio uses, not just one investment tool, but several tools to accomplish this. Just like those spinning plates, emphasis needs to be distributed to all your holdings, with no single one of them dominating to the neglect of the others.

Take dividend-producing stocks as an income source, for example. They can be excellent in their place, but if that is your sole strategy for retirement income, you could be in trouble if a bear market comes along and corporations begin reducing dividends because their industry fell on hard times.

A healthy portfolio is counterbalanced. The highway to financial failure is littered with the carcasses of those who put all their eggs in one basket. True diversification, as opposed to perceived diversification, is your best protection against financial failure.

Using Investment Tools

One of the best things North Carolina has going for it is its proximity to both the mountains and the coast. I am particularly blessed to live in the small town of Kernersville, which lies between the Atlantic Ocean and the Appalachian Mountains. There are just over 300 miles of shoreline in the Tar Heel state, and nearly every mile of it is accessible to the public. One of our family's favorite things to do is head for our little place at the beach when the weather is right.

The beach cottage takes all the hassle out of going to the beach. But our little "home away from home" also comes with some degree of upkeep and repair. As my wife, Belinda, will tell you, I am no handyman. If it's a serious repair, I call an expert. However, I keep a toolbox at the beach house for small jobs. In the toolbox are screwdrivers, a few wrenches, a socket set with a few pieces missing, a hammer, a measuring tape, and an assortment of nuts, bolts and screws that live in the bottom of the box (I hate to throw them out — just in case I ever need them).

While I am no expert in the use of these tools, it doesn't take a rocket scientist to figure out every tool has its purpose. I know this because I have wasted many hours of good sunshine trying to use the wrong tool for a specific job before finally breaking down and driving to the nearest hardware store to get the tool that fits the job. I may not be an expert handyman, but I have it on good authority that you don't use a pair of pliers to cut a board in half, or a handsaw to drive a nail into a plank. Now, does that mean either of those tools are no good? Of course not. Each is useful when used to do what they are designed to do.

It's like that with all the tools in the *investment toolbox*, which contains stocks, bonds, annuities, REITS, bank products, life insurance and the list goes on. Every tool has its purpose, depending on the financial objective.

Where people often go wrong is when they secure the services of a professional who only knows how to use one or two of these tools, or when they accept advice from a non-fiduciary who is only rewarded if you use the product he or she is selling. It reminds me of the line by famed psychologist Abraham Maslow published in "The Psychology of Science" in 1966: "I suppose it is tempting, if the only tool you have is a hammer, to treat everything as if it were a nail."

Asking a stockbroker about insurance will get you about as much information as asking an insurance agent about the stock market. A competent fiduciary, however, will know about both and advise you according to your needs, not what he or she has to sell.

CHAPTER TWELVE

Choosing the Right Financial Advisor for You

I have to hand it to Prudential Insurance Company for coming up with some entertaining and thoughtful ads in recent years about retirement. The theme for most of them is the dichotomy between how much people *think* they will need in retirement, and how much they will *actually* require.

In one recent ad they have seven couples lined up in a creative outdoor setting. Each couple is asked to punch into a screen how much money they will need in retirement. Apparently neither partner knows what figure the other enters. Then they walk onto what looks like a glass sidewalk that represents 30 years of life. Every step they take is a year. With each step, the square turns blue if they have enough money in that year. They know their projection was too low when they take a step and the square (year) blinks yellow. They just ran out of money.

The ones who guessed low seem embarrassed and shocked when they run out of money.

"Oh nooooo!" one man protests when he runs out of money after only six years. "How did this happen?"

"Are you going to leave me back here at year nine?" says a
woman to her husband after her square turns yellow and he continues walking on the blue.

It makes the point quite cleverly that most people don't have a
clue as to how much they will need to live a comfortable and carefree life in their golden years.

The sad truth about planning for retirement is that many people spend more time planning their two-week vacation than planning the rest of their lives. That shouldn't be the case, and it
doesn't have to be.

Seeking Professional Help

Two areas of life in which you should not (a) procrastinate or
(b) try to handle it alone are your **health** and your **wealth.** I know of
people who postponed seeking medical attention until it was too
late. Procrastination in that area can be just as harmful to your
health as putting off planning for your financial future can be to
your wealth.

It is risky to take a do-it-yourself approach to managing one's
financial future. I'm not talking about the casual investor who enjoys using a little "play money" to fund online trading in the stock
market. I have some clients who are completely self-taught, who
have become quite good at technical analysis. But they don't put
their life's savings on the line with these trades. By the same token,
I know others who failed miserably at online trading when they
didn't know when to back away from the computer.

General financial planning should be done with the help of
professionals who are fully trained and whose jobs require them to
keep up with economic trends. No sane individual would attempt
self-surgery or self-dentistry, yet too many DIY planners each year

will make expensive mistakes that could have been avoided with the help of a competent, experienced financial planner.

If you were to draw a timeline of your past, you would see the intersections where your life was impacted by a financial decision you either made or failed to make correctly. Going forward, making the wrong decision or making no decision at all could cost you financially to the tune of years of lost earnings, thousands of dollars in unnecessary taxes or missed opportunities.

If that makes the case for seeking professional help in this area of life, then I have succeeded. But these days, the woods are full of individuals claiming to be experts. How do you go about selecting the right financial advisor for you?

Selecting the Right Advisor

The interview process works well for this.

What do you mean, Robert?

Well, if you are going to place your confidence *and* potentially your life's savings in someone's care, you should know that individual both personally and professionally. No true professional will mind answering questions about their credentials and qualifications. In fact, they should welcome such inquiries. They should be glad to share with you how many years' experience they have, and tell you about their training and why they qualify to give you advice.

Ask, "Are you a fiduciary?" If they fidget or tap dance around the answer to that one, you may be in the wrong place. You are certainly in the wrong place if they respond, "What's a fiduciary?" As explained earlier in this book, this is a legal term requiring a financial advisor to put your interests ahead of their own in *all* matters.

It is one thing to hang out a shingle saying you are a "financial advisor." Almost anyone can do that these days. It is quite another to have years of experience and hundreds of client success stories behind you. Also, check out the candidate's business card. This is also not a perfect indicator of the candidate's credentials. Not all professionals put their certifications and designations on their business card, but most of them do. Do the letters after his or her name look like alphabet soup to you? Ask what the letters mean. If you don't understand each one, ask again until you understand. A qualified, competent professional will not mind this little interrogation.

Ask, "How are you paid?" While it may be considered impolite at a dinner party to ask such a question, this is — to quote a line from "The Godfather" — not personal; it's business. You aren't asking for their bank balance or net worth. You just want to know if there are any possible conflicts of interest. How financial advisors are paid may reveal the level of their objectivity when it comes to their recommendations.

No financial advisor works for free. But true fiduciaries are under obligation to recommend strategies and products irrespective of compensation.

Sometimes your choice of a financial advisor may boil down to whether they ask you enough questions. In our office, we train our advisors to explain investment options carefully, and then have clients explain it back to them — along with any fees — before letting them sign any paperwork. This gives clients confidence in their decision and enhances their understanding.

What type of questions would the right financial advisor for you ask? There are hundreds.

- Where do you see yourself in the next 5, 10, 15 years?
- What are your goals, your desires, your dreams?
- In detail, what do you want to do when you retire?

All manner of such questions should come before any financial analysis takes place. At Robert Cooper & Associates, we take pride in knowing our clients on a first-name basis, and we want to see them several times a year.

Ask, "What is your investing philosophy?" A true professional will probably not give you this answer without knowing what you want out of life. Why? Because their job is like that of a taxi driver. They want to take you where you want to go. You don't ask a taxi driver, "Where are you going?" It's the other way around. No competent physician will prescribe medicine before knowing everything about you and what other medication you are taking. Likewise, a fiduciary financial advisor will want to know many details about you before making any recommendations.

Asking, "What is your investment philosophy" is also a good way to smoke out a salesperson who views you as a cash cow. If the answer starts with a list of mutual funds or stocks he or she recommends based on a projected return, you know you are dealing with an accumulation specialist, not an advisor specializing in income planning.

Ask, "How will we work together?" This is the way you find out who your contact person at the firm will be. Who will actually manage your portfolio? You should have access to the firm's principal any time you wish. You will want to have a regularly scheduled conference with your financial team. Why is this important? Because tax laws change on a regular basis, and so does the economic landscape you are navigating. Your advisors are like the ones keeping watch from the masthead of a ship to alert you of an approaching storm. Good communication between you and your financial advisory team is crucial. Other qualifiers are: Do they understand taxes? Do they understand insurance? Are they capable of coordinating or working with your legal professionals to help you with wills, trusts and other legal documents?

In the end, do not fail to plan. In case you haven't heard it before, I will repeat the adage again: "Failing to plan is planning to fail." I believe it, though. It's true.

ROBERT D. COOPER

About the Author

Robert Cooper is an Investment Advisor Representative, a Chartered Retirement Planning Consultant and a Registered Financial Consultant at Robert Cooper & Associates in Kernersville, North Carolina. He grew up in Salisbury, North Carolina. In 1982, he graduated from Catawba College, earning his degree in business and economics.

Robert married Belinda Cooper in 1987.They are parents of a son, James Cooper, and daughter, Amanda Smith. He is the son of Clarence Cooper, who passed away in 1989, and Jenelle Cooper.

"I majored in business and economics in college because I had a vision of being self-employed," says Robert. Upon graduation, he went to work at Food Lion, a supermarket chain based in Salisbury, as a store manager, and was soon transferred to High Point to manage a store there.

In 1989, Robert began working in the insurance industry representing Life of Georgia in the Winston-Salem area. Shortly thereafter, he founded a property and casualty insurance agency in Greensboro.

While he was in the insurance business, Robert discovered he had a passion for helping people achieve their financial goals. He changed careers and obtained the credentials and education to qualify him as a financial advisor. He founded Robert Cooper & Associates in 1993.

Personal Life

Robert met his wife, Belinda, on a blind date. "You need to meet our Sunday school teacher," one of his cashiers at Food Lion told him. "It was arranged, and the rest is history," says Robert.

The Coopers love going for long weekends to the beach where they have a "little getaway" on Oak Island, just below Southport. Robert likes organized running and has participated in half-marathons, a 50k relay and a 5k event.

He belongs to Kernersville Wesleyan Church and enjoys working with other church members in support of missions in foreign countries. He has participated in several mission trips to Guatemala and finds satisfaction in giving to others.

"You think you know what poor is, but you don't really know until you meet some of these people," Robert says. Working with the church's "Happy Feet" program, Robert says he helped bring two cases of shoes to villages and towns where residents lived in huts with dirt floors.

"Just as we ran out of shoes, an elderly man showed up," Robert said. "He wore my size, so I gave him mine. Fortunately, I had another pair."

Robert said he and his wife have learned many valuable life lessons through his missionary outreach work. In 2013, while helping build a facility for missionaries, he received a real taste of what life is like in third-world countries.

"They have nothing," he said. "No paved streets, no trash pickup. Their drinking water is pumped from a lake — the same lake where they bathe and do their laundry. But they are proud people.

The challenge was to help them without robbing them of their dignity. We didn't want to make them feel embarrassed."

The Coopers believe in giving back to their local community. Along with clients of Robert Cooper & Associates, they recently spearheaded a food drive for Crisis Control Ministry, which donated more than 350 cans of food. In 2016, the firm sponsored Kernersville Cares for Kids.

Acknowledgments

I would like to express my gratitude to several people without whose help this project would not have been possible. First, Lou Blackman. Lou and I have worked together for the past eight years. In the office, he has seen me at my worst and my best. I never want to miss an opportunity to express to him how valuable he is to me, and how much I appreciate him. Also, I am grateful to my beautiful wife, Belinda Cooper. She has blessed me with 30 years of marriage and has always supported me no matter what my vision or plan was. I am such a much better person for having her in my life.

The most important acknowledgment goes to my Savior, Jesus Christ. He knows my imperfections and failures. He also knows I am still a work in progress.

Contact

If anything in this book resonated with you or if you'd like more information on ways to address retirement income concerns, feel free to contact my office:

<u>Robert Cooper & Associates</u>
935 East Mountain St., Suite E
Kernersville, NC 27284
(336) 993-2012 | robert@coopercares.com
http://www.coopercares.com

www.ingramcontent.com/pod-product-compliance
Lightning Source LLC
Chambersburg PA
CBHW070350220526
45467CB00001B/324